Pioneer Voices of Zion Canyon

Pioneer Voices *of* Zion Canyon

by Eileen M. Smith-Cavros

INTRODUCTION BY Lyman Hafen

PHOTOGRAPHS BY Michael Plyler

Zion Natural History Association
Zion National Park, Utah

Project managed by Lyman Hafen
Book design and composition by Sandy Bell
Photographs (unless otherwise noted)
by Michael Plyler
Printed in Singapore by Tien Wah Press

FRONT COVER: Alma Cox
FRONT ENDSHEET: Crawford family picnic in
Zion Canyon, March 1917. Far left, Elva
Crawford, Mrs. W. L. Crawford, W. L. Crawford,
Lloyd and LaDessa Crawford, and Ellen Bean. Seated
on upper rock, Uncle J. M. Bean and J. L. Crawford.
Photograph by William L. Crawford.
BACK ENDSHEET: Threshing wheat in Zion Canyon,
c. 1915. Bishop Thornton Hepworth at far right.
Photograph by William L. Crawford.
PAGE 1: Carnelia Crawford (seated) and daughters in
front of Walter Ruesch's 1926 Chevrolet.
PAGES 2-3: From left to right, J. L. with cat,
Lloyd, and Elva Crawford in the iris garden in
Oak Creek Canyon. Photograph by
William L. Crawford.
PAGE 5: top, Clara Cope; right, J. L. Crawford and
Elva Twitchell; bottom, Austen Excell.

CONTENTS

ACKNOWLEDGMENTS

THE NON-PROFIT ZION NATURAL HISTORY ASSOCIATION and the Zion Canyon Field Institute would like to thank the following for providing funding support for this project: the George S. and Dolores Dore Eccles Foundation, the Charles Redd Center for Western Studies and the Utah Humanities Council. The Utah Humanities Council promotes history and heritage, books and reading and public discussion of issues important to our communities.

We appreciate the long-standing and excellent relationship we enjoy with Zion National Park and wish to thank, in particular, Superintendent Jock Whitworth, Chief of Interpretation Ron Terry, Assistant Chief of Interpretation Tom Haraden, and Museum Curator Leslie Courtright, for their support of this project. We also thank the members of the ZNHA Board of Directors: Dr. Joseph Sharp, chairman; Bart Anderson, Pam Hilton, Nick Jorgensen, Roland Lee, James Lemmon, John W. Palmer, Curt Walker, and Paul Wilson.

Harvesting cane in Oak Creek, 1918. Photograph by William L. Crawford.

We would like to thank the following people who so graciously shared their time and their memories for this project and allowed volunteers to record their oral histories for the Pioneer Voices of Zion Canyon Project:

David Terry	Philip Hepworth
Vilo DeMille	Nora Flanigan Bradshaw
Oscar Johnson	Lorna Jolley Kesterson
Barbara Bell	Fae Terry Jenacaro
Evelyn Bleak	Yvonne Hoff
Shirl Pitchforth	Nellie Ballard
J. L. Crawford	Janis Kali
Elva Twitchell	Alma Cox
Clara Cope	Austen Excell
Della Higley	Drew Jennings
Lola Beatty Hirschi Campbell	Betsy Alford
LaDessa Miller	Dan Crawford

We would like to thank the following people who gave willingly of their time to perform and to transcribe interviews for the Pioneer Voices of Zion Canyon Project:

Dan McGuire	Vicki Parkinson
Alison Keith	Sarah Horton
Lynne Cobb	Tracy Jones
Bob Jones	Lyman Hafen
Greer Chesher	Victor Hall
Kurtis Jones	Elizabeth Schroder
Kristin Jones	Skip Piper

Complete copies of all transcripts and all photographs are available for researchers. Copies will be stored at the Zion National Park archives and at Dixie State College.

J. L. Crawford, born 1914, in front of Steamboat Mountain
(The West Temple)

In the Shadow
of Steamboat Mountain

by Lyman Hafen

*No place is a place until things that
have happened in it are remembered in history,
ballads, yarns, legends or monuments.*

—WALLACE STEGNER

A LARGE RECTANGLE OF SANDSTONE, the size of a closet, lies next to the road not far inside the south gate of Zion National Park. I pass that rock every morning on my way to the office. Until recently it was nothing more to me than another piece of loose stone scattered along the canyon floor. Had I ever thought to make the connection, I might have deduced that the rock fell away from a ridge of the Springdale Member of the Moenave Formation where it juts out to a point a few hundred feet above the road. I never made the connection until it was made for me by a 92-year-old man as we drove past it in my car.

"That's the nose of the Zion Sphinx," the man said.

I did a double-take over my shoulder as we drove on down the road. When I asked for an explanation, the man, whose name is J. L. Crawford, told me the story. J. L. was born in 1914, not far from that rock, in Oak Creek Canyon at the foot of the Temples and Towers of the Virgin. My office sits on what was once Crawford property. I park my car in a lot that was once the Crawford Family orchard. And when I sit at my desk I can

LEFT: J. L. Crawford at about 15 (1929) with the Zion Sphinx in the background. Photograph by William L. Crawford.

RIGHT: J. L. Crawford in front of the same ledge that now resembles the profile of his father's face, July 2006. Photograph by Michael Plyler.

look up and out a window that perfectly frames Oak Creek Canyon, a view considered by many as the most outstanding skyline on Planet Earth. For J. L. Crawford it is simply the backyard of his boyhood universe.

From the south window of my office is a wonderful view of the Springdale Sandstone ridge from which fell the aforementioned rock. It takes only a little imagination to see the profile of an old man's face at the point of the ridge—a kind of Zion Sphinx. When J. L. was a boy living beneath that ledge in the 1920s, the artist J. B. Fairbanks had dubbed it "The Sphinx." When J. L. came home from World War II in 1945, the rock that had formed the large nose in the profile had fallen away and found its angle of repose on the canyon floor. The rockfall distinctly transformed the ledge's profile into an uncanny resemblance to the face of J. L.'s father, William L. Crawford. To the millions of visitors who, over the last half-century, have driven past that solitary rock along the road, it is just another large boulder among hundreds strewn across the canyon floor. To me, now that I know the story, the rock is a link that connects the exterior physical landscape with the landscape of imagination inside me. When story and place connect in such a manner, the landscape is enlivened. It becomes much more than just a pretty scene. It becomes a part of you.

Such connections can be made in many ways. For some, the Zion story that resonates deepest is its geology—an epic that hurtles you back through the ages to a time when this landscape resided near the Equator and thousands of feet of desert sand were deposited by dry winds and by the transgression and recession of great seas and flood

Oak Creek Village, 1929, photograph by William L. Crawford. The nearest home in the foreground is where the Zion National Park Human History Museum is now located.

plains. For others, it is the story of the Virgin River, the persistent stream that carved the canyon and continues its inexorable rush to the ocean today, the same river that makes the canyon a verdant sanctuary for a phenomenal variety of plants and animals. Still others make their most significant connection to this landscape through the story of the ancient human inhabitants who left hints of their lives pecked in the rocks. Subtle signs remain of the Ancestral Puebloans who lived here more than a thousand years ago, and the Southern Paiutes who resided along the river they called Pa'rus when Anglo settlers arrived in the mid 1800s.

When we began the Pioneer Voices Project in 2004, our goal was to capture a quickly vanishing chapter of the Zion story. Much has been written and recorded of the geology, the flora and fauna, the river habitat, the ancient inhabitants, the Southern Paiutes, and the early Anglo settlers of the Zion Canyon area. But a gap exists between the frontier history and the modern times in which we live. It is a gap that begins about the time J. L. Crawford was born and continues through the 1920s, and 30s, the years in which Zion National Park was discovered by the world, the years during which the canyon transformed from a place where settlers eked out a meager living along the river, to a destination where travelers from every quadrant of the globe come to be inspired and renewed by the sight of unfathomable scenic wonder. We set about to fill that gap with the oral histories of more than two dozen wonderful people who lived in or near the canyon at some point during those years. These are special people whose lives link us with the frontier this place once was, and whose stories connect us with the landscape in ways that enliven it in our minds.

Wallace Stegner wrote, "A place is not a place until people have been born in it, have grown up in it, lived in it, known it, died in it—have both experienced and shaped it, as individuals, families, neighborhoods, and communities, over more than one genera-tion." An important part of the mission of Zion Natural History Association is to help visitors to Zion National Park develop a "sense of place" for this region. That sense of place begins with a knowledge as shallow as simply being able to point to where it is on a map. From there it grows deeper as one delves into the history, which can take you back 250 million years to the Jurassic, Triassic and Permian Periods. But a truly authentic sense of place can only be gained when one has lived in a place long enough to shed a lifetime's worth of blood, sweat and tears upon it—to have lived through its round of seasons, known the nuances of its morning winds and evening breezes, eaten from its soil and from the flesh of the animals that ate its plants. Though it would be impossible for us in this modern age to develop such a sense for Zion Canyon, we are fortunate to still have among us many wonderful people who possess just that. The Pioneer Voices Project was undertaken to document and preserve for posterity the marvelous sense of place harbored in this select group of people.

Most folks I know vividly recall their first encounter with Zion National Park. It is one of those seminal moments in a life that imprints itself on the soul. For many of those interviewed in the Pioneer Voices Project, that first encounter with the canyon was

The John Crawford farm in Oak Creek Village, 1919. Photograph by Shiplers.

simultaneous with the first breaths of life. This was the landscape through which they came into consciousness. Stegner writes of the profound effect the landscape of childhood can exert on a person. "Expose a child to a particular environment at his susceptible time and he will perceive in the shapes of that environment until he dies," he wrote. The powerful forms of Zion's towers of stone have indelibly shaped the psyche of each of these canyon natives.

On the same day J. L. Crawford and I drove past the nose of the Sphinx near the south entrance to the park, we also drove up the switchbacks of State Road 9 toward the Zion-Mt. Carmel Tunnel. My earliest memories of Zion include the almost otherwordly experience of winding up those switchbacks in our 1950s Ford sedan. I craned my neck as my father pointed to the windows in the sheer canyon wall and explained that soon we would enter a mile-long tunnel. Up the switchbacks we chugged, the car choking

From left to right: Victor Ruesch, Verl Russell, and school teacher Bert Sullivan, 1925, in front of what is now Zions Bank in Springdale. Photograph by William L. Crawford.

and lurching as we drew ever nearer that mystical place where the road disappeared into the mountain. My heart raced as the canyon wall swallowed us whole and we floated into darkness. Dad switched on the lights and rolled down the windows and the dank sandstone air came at us in a rhythmic beat as we zoomed past the tunnel's concrete columns. Then Dad laid into the horn and it rang in the darkness until its shrill bark pierced our souls. When he finally let up, the trailing echo continued to ring in my ears. It rings still, these decades later. It is a very real remnant of childhood, a palpable link to those magical moments deep inside the Navajo Sandstone of Zion National Park.

As J. L. and I drove up the switchbacks that day not long ago, he asked me to pull off at a certain spot well up the side of the canyon. We got out of the car and headed onto a sandy terrace dotted with juniper trees and brush. We walked through a brisk, easy breeze and J. L. pointed out where various buildings such as the bunk houses and the kitchen had stood. This had been the site of the Nevada Camp, where the workers who built the tunnel in the late 1920s had lived. J. L. had been a boy in his early and mid teens during those monumental years. He lived on a humble farm down canyon, beneath all the hubbub of construction. He befriended the stepson of the project's superintendent, a boy named Johnny Doane. The two of them spent countless hours roaming the talus slopes and scaling the ledges beneath the slowly progressing tunnel.

I was overwhelmed by a sense of grandeur as we stood on that magnificent terrace. Sheer sandstone walls towered above us; the floor of the canyon lay far below. It was difficult to imagine that a village had once stood there, suspended on a small shelf on the canyon's face. J. L. walked about in his matter-of-fact manner, showing me where the superintendent's house had stood, where Johnny's mother had fed him meals, and then—stopping at a certain spot between two juniper trees—he said, "This is right about where I had my tonsils removed."

"What?"

J. L. went on to explain that one day in 1929, when he was in 9th grade, he came down with a terribly sore throat. His parents took him to the nearest doctor, which happened to be Doc McIntyre, the camp physician at the Nevada Camp. The doctor diagnosed J. L. with tonsillitis. He laid the boy out right there in his office next to the superintendent's house on the edge of a cliff in Zion Canyon, put him under with ether, and removed his tonsils.

There I stood, on a breeze-swept terrace midway up the canyon wall, on the very spot where the 92-year-old man who stood next to me had undergone surgery as a boy. The story was from another time, an era so far removed from my frame of reference I could hardly imagine it. But the place where the story occurred remains. I will never pass that place again without remembering the story.

Later that morning J. L. and I walked up Oak Creek Canyon, winding our way through the soft chatter of cottonwood leaves. We walked through the foreground of the scene framed by my office window. J. L. pointed to the right at a small draw between talus slopes fanning to the canyon floor. "That's Cougar Holler," he said. "Once a cougar killed a dog and deposited its remains up there." The next draw to the west he identified as Balsam Holler. Then we came to what he called Oak Flat where there is now park service employee housing. Then Sage Flat, which is now the park's maintenance yard. None of these names have ever appeared on an official map. J. L. drew my attention to the handsome stone buildings in the maintenance yard and reminded me they had been built by the boys of the Civilian Conservation Corps during the Depression in the mid 1930s. He also reminded me he had been one of those CCC boys and he had dressed some of the stone blocks in those buildings. If he took the time and looked hard enough, he mused, he could probably put his finger on some of the very stones he shaped.

As we stood near the split of Left Hand Fork and Right Hand Fork in Oak Creek Canyon, we looked back down to the east and J. L. swept his arm across the 360 acres his family had owned when he was a boy. The delightful, trickling stream called Oak Creek ran through the middle of it. Only 14 acres had been suitable for farming. Most of the rest was too vertical or rocky. He showed me remnants of irrigation ditches, some of which I see every day out my office window, and expressed how much he loathed cleaning those ditches as a boy. He showed me where the ice pond had been, the magical place that lingered most of the day in canyon shadows, where the Crawfords extracted ice during the colder months of the year. As we walked back down toward my office he showed me where the barn had been that housed the cow he milked every morning before school, where the hay field had been where he and his brothers cut and raked hay into winrows, then stacked it in haycocks, then ultimately pitched it onto a horse-drawn wagon and hauled it to the barn. He showed me where his father's raspberry patch had been, where the various varieties of fruit trees had grown, all those exotic trees sprouted from seeds ordered from catalogs.

J. L. showed me the place on the hill where he and his brother Lloyd stood look-out for cars coming into the canyon. The first automobile had appeared in Zion in 1915, when J. L. was but a year old. For a long time the sight of a car was a novelty for the Crawford boys, but as they grew into their teens, traffic into the canyon increased, and with it increased the boys' ability to identify the make and model of every car they spied.

Oak Creek Village, 1920, photograph by William L. Crawford.

The brothers poured through magazines and newspapers and memorized the profile of each car model. They maintained an ongoing competition to see who was fastest and most accurate at naming the Packard, the Nash or the Model A that chugged up the dusty road into the canyon.

Their father had been an amazing combination of farmer, technician and artist. He kept a darkroom in their humble house and over the years produced hundreds of black and white photographs of the canyon. J. L. and Lloyd supplemented the family income by hailing cars as they rumbled past the house and selling photos to the visitors for a nickel apiece. I tried to imagine two sandy-haired, barefoot boys in bib overalls, their skinny arms outstretched with photos as they approached those strangers behind the big wheels of their idling cars.

As J. L. and I finished our walk that morning, he realized we were standing near what was once his father's watermelon patch. It brought to mind another story. His father, like most of the other residents of Zion Canyon in those days, was a devout Mormon, a member of the Church of Jesus Christ of Latter-day Saints. The Crawford Family joined in prayer morning and night, expressing gratitude to God for their blessings and petitioning the simple things they needed to sustain their lives in the canyon. "In those prayers my father always used to say: 'Bless the water and the elements,'" J. L. recalled. "When I was very young I thought he was saying: 'Bless the watermelons.' I figured my father had a lot of pull with the Lord because his watermelons were always the best."

Standing in the stark, mid-day sun, surrounded by towering spires of Navajo Sandstone, a line from a Barry Lopez story streamed through my mind. "Everything is held together with stories," he wrote. "That is all that is holding us together, stories and compassion." I felt grateful for the stories I'd been given that day. Each one was a gleaming gem. Each one tied me ever more tightly to this place called Zion. I thought of J. L. and his family in the early years of the twentieth century, how they struggled to survive in this wondrous side canyon of Zion. How every day was another round of give and take with nature. How they lived at the gate of what became Mukuntuweap National Monument in 1909, and then Zion National Park in 1919. How, by the 1930s, the park had become so popular the federal government wanted to buy their farm and make it the entrance to the park. How J. L., by then a college student, was torn between losing his boyhood home and the realization that there was not really a stable future in the canyon for him, anyway. What's more, he was tired of cleaning ditch and pitching hay and milking cows. He, like many other canyon natives of his generation, had set his sights beyond the magnificent Zion horizon. I also thought of how J. L.'s grandmother, the matriarch of the canyon at the time the Crawford Farm was sold to the government, was heart-broken when the sale went through. "Why don't they just knock me in the head and leave me here," she said when it was time to go.

I'm sitting in my office looking out my window and up at the West Temple of Zion. It stands a magnificent 3,800 feet above the canyon floor. On a modern map, "West Temple" is its official name. For most of the millions of visitors who come to Zion each

Springdale Schoolhouse class group, c. 1928. The teacher in the last row, left, is Lillian Atkin.

year, "West Temple" is as far as it goes. But there is more to know. The old-timers called it Steamboat Mountain. The Southern Paiutes and the Ancestral Puebloans before them surely had names for it as well, though I am sad to say I do not know them.

The Pioneer Voices Project is meant to open our eyes to that chapter of the Zion story when the West Temple was known as Steamboat Mountain. It was a time when a select few people were born in the canyon, grew up in it, lived in it, knew it, and shaped it as individuals, families, and a community, over more than one generation. Their lives are a part of the canyon's natural history. Their stories hold the power to connect us to this place in a special way.

Pioneer Voices of Zion Canyon

by Eileen M. Smith-Cavros

Zion Pioneers and Nature

THE CHILDREN AND GRANDCHILDREN of the Mormon pioneers who set-tled in Zion Canyon during the latter decades of the nineteenth century shared common struggles and joys with those who preceded them. New challenges arose as well. Their relationships with the land, the Virgin River and the animals around them, as well as the development of a national park in their "backyard," reflected tradition *and* transition in many ways. These second and third generation set-tlers were interviewed for the "Pioneer Voices of Zion Canyon" project in 2004. They recalled their youth in the land of Zion, along the banks of the river and against the backdrop of Navajo Sandstone, as a central and formative part of their lives.

These children who grew up in the greater Zion area from the 1910s to the 1930s witnessed the discovery of their haven by the "outside" world. They watched as the "first million-dollar mile" of United States highway ever built (Garate 2004) connected the west side of Zion with the east. These children saw the populations of once-common

FAE TERRY JENACARO, BORN 1917

animals decline, while other animals they had rarely seen, multiplied. The people who dispensed medicine to them when they were ill changed from mothers and midwives to small-town doctors. Some watched as their grandparents reluctantly sold their Zion homesteads to the federal government. Others watched as their parents struggled each year, attempting to farm through the alternating droughts and floods that are still characteristic cycles along the banks of the Virgin River.

The memories that interviewees in the "Pioneer Voices" project shared are a valuable source of information. They help to explain how the families of Zion settlers used, changed, valued and battled with the nature and the resources that surrounded them. Delving into how these Zion pioneers viewed the natural world is more than an exercise in cultural preservation. In looking at yesterday and gaining a better understanding of the heritage and history of the interplay between people and natural resources, we may learn information that will help us better understand the present state of the ecosystem. Many of the descendants of the original settlers still reside in southern Utah. Their own histories have influenced the way they feel about the natural world today.

Zion National Park is a treasure of the United States and, indeed, the world. Its geological monuments, wilderness, and vast biodiversity do not exist in isolation from the human world that surrounds it. This has been true for thousands of years, since the first Native American "pioneers" entered the canyon, until the time of these nineteenth and twentieth century pioneers and their children. Today 2.6 million visitors a year marvel at Zion. Some contemporary visitors, armed with G.P.S. units and climbing gear, reach places that earlier pioneers never dreamed of going. Despite the differences in their backgrounds, in their objectives and in the technology available to Zion's inhabitants and visitors across the years, one thing remains constant. Zion Canyon has impacted *Homo sapiens*, and they have impacted it; this exchange continues.

Those interviewed for this Pioneer Voices Project had varied youthful experiences and backgrounds. Some of their families owned land that eventually became a part of Zion National Park while others lived in the nearby "gateway" communities of Springdale and Rockville, Utah. All of the interviewees were over 60 years old, with most being in their 70s or 80s and a few were over 90 years old. All were raised in large Mormon families, with most still being active members of the Church of Jesus Christ of Latter-day Saints (LDS). A few had parents who worked in Zion National Park. Some interviewees had worked in the park themselves. Several had pioneer parents who owned businesses and their upbringings were fairly stable financially, while others came from more challenging economic circumstances including families that were landless renters. Most of their families, however, had orchards, gardens, or farms and grew or collected at least part, if not most, of their food at some time between 1910–1930. Many of the interviewees recounted that their parents or grandparents were sent to the Zion Canyon area as part of the "Cotton Mission" by LDS President Brigham Young or as part of a later church colonizing mission.

The Dixie Cotton Mission in the 1860s was a difficult assignment given out by the expanding LDS church. Families who were called to southern Utah met an inhospitable land with less-than-fertile soil. Rain was a feast or famine proposition as the Native Americans (Ancestral Puebloans and later Paiutes) had discovered years before, making agriculture a challenge. The typical experience of Zion's earliest Mormon settlers was not unlike that detailed by Victor Hall, an interviewer for the Pioneer Voices Project who himself was a descendant of Zion-area settlers. In his compilation, a *History of Rockville* (Hall 1999) he retold:

> Kezia, beautiful, twenty years old and out of work, was encouraged to find a family that was reasonably secure financially and, if mutually agreeable, marry the husband. Thirty-eight-year-old John Charles fell way short of meeting the financial criterion but Kezia did respect him and she wanted to assist Selena [John's first wife] who now had three children. The marriage took place in the Salt Lake endowment house September 17, 1857. John and his families were called to the Dixie cotton mission in 1861. They first settled in Adventure, now the west end of Rockville. Restricted acreage and flooding soon caused the abandonment of Adventure. The families moved to higher ground in the new town of Rockville, named in honor of the huge boulders found there (p. 4).

The life of many first generation Zion pioneers reflected this pattern of settlement, flood, and resettlement. The towns of Grafton, Adventure, Duncan's Retreat, Northrop, and Shunesburg, all near Zion Canyon, became ghost towns within years or decades after first settlement due to varied incidents ranging from flood to altercations with Native Americans. After a generation, however, most pioneers who remained found a place they considered "home." They attempted to homestead far enough from the Virgin River to prevent flooding during most years, yet close enough to the river for easy access to what became their drinking and irrigation water for many years.

The following sections address the ways in which the progeny of these pioneers recalled the natural world of their youth. Their parents and grandparents had arrived in an ecosystem which held plants, soil, climate patterns, animals and natural resource issues that were unfamiliar to them. By the 1910s, many Zion Canyon families had set patterns of natural resource use in response to the ecosystem. Some of their environmental choices and attitudes reflected what we might consider "wise-use" of resources today, while other choices strained the natural system.

Interviewee Della Higley, resident of Springdale for more than eight decades, shared memories that embodied many of the stories recorded and archived for this project:

My mother and father were married in 1898, and they had eight children. We lived in a small home . . . I don't remember exactly how many rooms. I think there were only two. And our heat was the fireplace . . . we had a small wood stove . . . My Uncle Dan lived on the same little hill, only just a ways up from us. My grandmother and Uncle Johnny lived on the next little hill down below us . . . grandmother had a large home, and she and Aunt Emma lived there, 'cause my grandfather had died before I was born . . . Well, grandmother moved to Shunesburg, where her family stayed. And grandfather came down [from] Draper; he built one of the first two houses that were built in Rockville. He decided that he wanted to move up toward the end of the canyon—he didn't want to live near the springs because of the mosquitoes. So he bought five acres of land and then he filed on other land. The land was poor so he . . . when it would rain he would turn the water out on to his land and he built the soil up to where it was good soil for farming. We would have parties, we would have dances, and we would go up into the canyon and have picnics. And at night, we would sit around the fireplace and tell stories, or sing to the tune of the organ or the harmonica. My father made a contraption so you could play the harmonica and organ at the same time . . . On Sunday we would walk to Sunday school in the morning and walk back home again, which was two miles. Then in the afternoon, we would walk to church and then back home. Then at night we would go down to the Mutual. . . . We were taught in the home to live our religion, and to love one another . . . We loved the land and we love the park and we felt that the land should be taken care of and not destroyed.

This closeness to the land should not simply be romanticized by modern observers, but examined realistically. While there was indeed a love of the land of Zion evidenced in the Pioneer Voices interviews, the interviewees also related how life in southern Utah during the early twentieth century was a constant tug-of-war between resources and people. Farming, livestock and daily life in Zion Canyon meant encounters from rattle-snakes to crop failure, from biting insects to mountain lion attacks on sheep, from the illness of children to floods that washed away bridges and buildings. Other disheartening events ranged from fatal lightning strikes, rock falls and locust swarms to the relative annoyances of muddy drinking water, late freezes and the condition known as "Virgin River bloat." Life was a daily struggle. Some settlers, dismayed by the challenges, returned to the more populous and "civilized" Wasatch Front in northern Utah. Given irrigation difficulties, unfamiliar cold desert terrain, the relatively infertile soil, drastic climate cycles, and the remoteness of Zion Canyon in the late nineteenth to early twentieth century, it is perhaps surprising that so many settlers stayed and persevered.

The fact that the early settlers had a "religious calling" to Zion undoubtedly contributed to their tenacity in difficult circumstances. One must also consider, viewing Zion today, that its rugged splendor was among the factors that convinced many to stay when there were easier lives and more accessible resources to be had elsewhere. Indeed, many of the pioneers interviewed for this project have never left Zion, while others live elsewhere, yet still describe it as "home."

While interviewing 94-year-old Elva Twitchell, born in Zion in 1910, the following exchange took place:

INTERVIEWER: "You lived [in Springdale] until . . . ?"
TWITCHELL: "Still here!"
INTERVIEWER: "But you live in Henderson [Nevada] now, don't you?"
TWITCHELL: "I'm staying with my son, that's why. But I still figure this is my home."

Another interviewee Fae (Terry) Jenacaro, born in 1917 in Rockville, grew up to become one of the first female dentists in the western United States and she has traveled the world. She commented, "I was always telling [people] what a beautiful country [southern Utah] is . . . they should go see it. When I've been other places and they have all these trees right down to the road . . . they're beautiful for a little while. But when you get to the point where that's all you can see is green trees, you can't see any distance, you can't see any color, you can't see any mountains, then I long for seeing southern Utah." Exploring the connections between these settlers, their families and the land of Zion may help to explain some of that longing.

Zion Pioneers and Plants

THE DIVERSITY OF FLORA found in southern Utah is a surprise to many newcomers. However, ecologically, this variety of plants is to be expected since the area of Zion National Park and its surroundings is the place where the Great Basin and the Mojave Desert meet the Colorado Plateau. It is a transition zone replete with diversity, and Zion National Park alone is home to over 900 species of plants. Drastic changes in the elevation of the area also characterize different plant

ELVA TWITCHELL, BORN 1910

communities. By traveling from the west to the east side of Zion, the visitor gains over 3,000 feet in elevation in 30 minutes. One is able to enjoy orchids, cacti, pine trees, lilies, oaks, ferns, maples and spectacular sub-alpine wildflowers all in a single day. The beauty and variety of the native plant species was not lost on the pioneers. Alder and Brooks (1996) retell the tale of a depressed pioneer bride whose husband convinced her to stay in "barren" unsettled Utah with his gift of a wild Sego lily (p. 79). In addition to aesthetics, however, the plants of the region provided early inhabitants of Zion with sustenance and medicine.

By the second and third generation, the dependency of Zion Canyon settlers on plants gathered in the wild had declined from earlier days. Children whose parents ran small local businesses or worked in the national park seemed to have less economic reliance on wild-gathered plants. Many families had also become more proficient at the "art" of agriculture in the desert, and as a result had more domestic plant sources for their needs and didn't have to rely as much on wild sources for food or medicine. Pioneers, using both dry-farming and irrigation, coaxed fruit, nuts and vegetables from the desert landscape. Although St. George and Hurricane, the nearest larger towns, were still a long day's journey away, supplies available there also likely led to decreased reliance on wild plants. In addition, as Zion National Park developed, regulations began to forbid the gathering of certain resources. However, most Pioneer Voices Project interviewees still reported the collection and use of select plants and plant products.

The use of certain wild plants for food sources was common for some families as evidenced by an interviewee who reported:

Pigweed [or] Lamb's quarters. We'd cook it. And sometimes we'd cook dandelion greens. They're so bitter you have to parboil them and pour the water off of them and then cook them tender. And we did turnip greens the same way . . . they made jelly of [cactus fruit]. I never did. I tried it once and all I could get was a handful of slivers. But my sister made it a lot.

Her brother also remembered eating Pigweed and noted "I think it was by choice. I don't know that we had to. And evidently it was plentiful and everybody liked it. I was never that crazy about so-called 'greens' and of course they'd boil them up and we'd just put vinegar on them and eat them." He also related bringing wild watercress to his future in-laws when he was "courting" his bride-to-be:

I used to take her family watercress and boy they liked that. We'd gather that down by the big spring pond. You know near the Switchback Restaurant in Springdale. Did you ever go to that big pond? I guess it still exists, I don't know. But when I was a kid it was owned by Freeborn Gifford and that's where the big spring was [from] which Springdale gets its name . . . where it drained out below, a big field of swampy area watercress and we'd just go and cut that stuff. We would gobble that and eat it with our bread and milk. You know. There'd be people making sandwiches out of it.

Several interviewees reported that the most commonly gathered wild plant in their childhood was wild asparagus and that it grew in area irrigation ditches as late as the 1980s:

Asparagus grew all over this place until I started leasing that pasture to horses. I can about 24 quarts a year offen my field as well as we ate it all the time . . . by this time it's gone to seed. But during the season we'd have a lot of asparagus. Oh! I've had a time trying to raise asparagus here since it quit growing wild up on the fields. I've planted up around the house here. Around the trees. I don't know why. I think they don't get the water they used to. And I know wild horses was in the pastures drinking the water. The guy that was irrigating here didn't know how to irrigate the way they used to do . . . and horses probably tromped it out too.

Some interviewees also mentioned commonly eating a plant they said resembled a wild onion or garlic as late as the 1930s. Austen Excell explained, "They used to even

LaDessa Miller, born 1916

eat what they called Bottle-stopper. . . . It's like an onion. It grows out of the ground and you pull it up and it's like a small onion on it. There's a hill up there we used to call Bottle-Stopper Hill. . . . Probably it tasted more like an onion, but it wasn't as strong as an onion. Green sprout, like an onion. If we had a good wet spring, they'd come up, a lot of them."

Interviewees frequently mentioned gathering wild berries as a distinct childhood memory, from serviceberries, to chokecherries and elderberries (Hall 1999, p. 30) to wild strawberries. Pioneer J. L. Crawford, a Zion ranger in the 1940s and a historian of the Zion Canyon area said:

> I remembered people talking about chokecherries. And elderberries. My dad used to talk about 'sarvice' berries. They didn't call them serviceberries; they called them 'sarvice' berries. But never did I see any of those maturing in Zion . . . and then chokecherries. People'd like to get those to make jelly out of them. They were excellent. My mother [made] some of the best jelly I ever ate [which] was a mixture of chokecherry and apple juice, mix them half and half. Made super jelly. Elderberries of course, they're always popular for jelly. And there again, you had to get up a little higher than the floor of Zion Canyon, and you had to get out on the plateau to gather any of those.

Crawford also remembered a place in Zion National Park named after the berries that grew there:

> There's a place in Zion called Raspberry Bend . . . That's the other side of Angels Landing. There's a big bend in the river, and on the shady side of the Organ [formation] between there and Angels Landing, in that cove, raspberries use to grow wild in there. As kids, we'd get in there . . . I didn't do it many times. But once in awhile, I'd get in there . . . we'd pick wild raspberries. They didn't grow in abundance. Where the parking area is on that point . . . the viewpoint for the Great White Throne. You know where you come to that very sharp

point, there's a turn out there, there's a plaque explaining the Great White Throne. Just right across the river...it's a shaded cove in there. [It's also called] Lime Kiln Point. [The raspberries there] they'd be different colors you know in there where it's shaded. Now [my folks] used to grow these black raspberries. But up there I don't know whether they were originally a black raspberry or a red one, but we'd find them all colors, even yellow sometimes. And I assume because they grow in the shade, they lacked the sunlight and didn't color up like they should be ... They were tasty. But no, they didn't grow in abundance enough to gather.

In spite of the LDS church prohibition on alcohol, many southern Utah settlers came from a European tradition of wine-making. "Wine-making in the home was a common practice throughout Dixie" (Hall 1999, p. 22). Some was sold to non-Mormons, some was imbibed at home, and according to Alder and Brooks (1996), wine was also produced for sacramental use (pp. 157–158). Grapes were also gathered for preserves. There is a native wild grape in Zion known as canyon grape, and some Mormon converts also cultivated exotic grape species with success. The following story retold by 92-year-old Della Higley described how the experience of gathering grapes in the wild was sometimes a hazardous one. This story also demonstrated how overcoming the hardships of nature was often actively connected to their own spirituality by the pioneers:

I'll tell you a story about when my cousin Sarah Winder Crawford was 10 years old. Her aunt lived in Virgin [Utah] and she sent word that there was lots of grapes ... so Uncle Sammy was going to take them ... but he made barrels for molasses for different people and he got word that the man he was making barrels for needed some and he couldn't go ... So just before [the women and children] get to Virgin, where they had to cross the river ... it was dangerous because one side of the crossing was rocky, the other quicksand ... the women kept saying "Well you drive [the wagon] across this place." And the other woman would say, "No you drive across it." Well, the horses soon found out that it wasn't a man driving so they just poked along. And it was dark before they got [to that place]. They decided the only thing they could do was to have a prayer. So they stopped and had prayer that the Lord would help them across this place. When they got to that place there was two shining lines across that river. And they crossed the river on these lines and looked back and there was no shining, no indication that the lines had ever been there. But they crossed in safety and went down and got their grapes. And that's why they got the grapes canned.

In addition to their use as food, Elva Twitchell also reported the use of several wild plants for medicinal purposes:

They used burdock root and blue cohosh, most of that you'd definitely have to go on the mountain for, and pennyroyal . . . Well, they used juniper berries for kidneys and that and we [now] find out that's not good. And I've been trying to think what they used that burdock . . . But the blue cohosh, they used it for heart and nerves. Pennyroyal was used for nerves and I think they used it for female problems too . . . Up on the East Rim [of Zion], they'd gather stuff up there. Course they didn't go up there for that until they got the [Zion] tunnel. It was too far around! It was a hundred miles from here to Orderville by going around through Colorado City and up through the sand. They couldn't go through the sand in the summer. They'd go in the winter when it was damp and still hard enough they could cross it. Otherwise they had to go clear down around by Pipe Spring [Arizona]. It was a big trip.

As Twitchell noted, the construction of the Zion Tunnel for the National Park Service in the late 1920s by the Nevada Contracting Company actually made it easier to travel and collect certain plants. The east side of Zion, at a higher altitude than the west, includes many plant species not found in the main canyon and the Zion Tunnel provided a more direct route. While plants were often sought after for medical needs, some pioneers also described less utilitarian uses of them:

Wreaths [were made] with [piñon] pine. And our gum came from pine trees; we'd chew pine gum. Then some of them made salve out of the sticky gum before it would harden. My neighbor would still make that once and awhile now. Her recipe come from Switzerland! Her grandmother came from Switzerland and she uses her recipe . . . We cut the flowers to decorate the graves. We didn't go buy flowers; silk flowers we didn't have. We'd just gather some out of the hills and out of our gardens.

Other Zion Canyon area residents also related childhood memories filled with flowers. "Many beautiful wild flowers grew on the hills at Crystal. I kept our mantelpiece filled with cans of Indian paintbrush, Sego lilies, Blue Bells and the sweet smelling wild rose" (Hall 1999, p. 32). One Pioneer Voices interviewee reminisced about his 1920s childhood playtime when children made necklaces from dandelions. "Take a stem of a dandelion and split it. And, weave another one through it. Make long chains." He continued on to describe:

We'd go cut pussy willows and make bouquets out of them . . . There were swampy areas along the Virgin River that had a lot of bulrushes and cattails and that sort of thing. This reminds me, too. I used to . . . when I was courting this gal one thing that helped me get her . . . win her was taking her bouquets of pussy willows. And where I'd gather those, going from Zion to Panguitch up there just above Glendale there's a little . . . well right below . . . Hidden Lake there [was] quite a big thicket of willows. At a certain time of the year there'd just be gobs of those pussy willows. I'd stop and cut a few sprigs off and take it to her.

Another interviewee described gathering wildflowers as a favorite childhood pastime in the 1930s:

I spent a lot of time outside. I especially loved the hills in front of my place. I could wander the hills and go all the way down to my Aunt Geneva Johnson's who lived right back of where the Shell station is now; just climb the hills! Looking for wildflowers. I loved to look for wildflowers, Sego lilies and Indian paintbrush and Slippery elm [orange-colored mallow], and Lady slippers and there were a lot of them around then. We'd go up on the hill and make play houses in among the sagebrush. I remember that my brother just older than I and my best girlfriend and her brother used to go up on the hill just in front of my folk's place and we made a little house amongst the sagebrush. And the boys had brought some rocks and built a little fire thing and we brought some hamburger and some potatoes and a frying pan and we'd cook our supper up on the hill. Got a lotta sand in it, but it tasted awful good! And we used to do that quite a bit.

While plants were recognized for their beauty, more interviewees discussed how those plants were primarily valued for their uses. Salves, for example, were an important traditional folk remedy for many early settlers. In Victor Hall's *History of Rockville* (1999) one of his interviewees described the treatment for a victim of a bear attack in the area:

At the cabin they fixed a pallet on the floor for him to lie on and dressed the wounds with the primitive materials available. Treatments consisted of washing the leg in broth from wild sage. Mary also made broth from oak and chokeberry bark for soaking. The bear was skinned and Mary rendered oil from it. Mixing some bear grease with sugar and balsam gum, she made a salve that she thought the best she had ever used (p. 36).

The pioneers utilized some plants in the same way the contemporary Paiutes did, so it is likely that some of the information was passed from the Native Americans to the

NELLIE BALLARD, BORN 1931

Mormon settlers (Larsen 2004, p. 69). Some Rockville families, for whom coffee and tea were prohibited by the church's "Word of Wisdom," made "Brigham's tea" from the Mormon tea plant. It was considered medicinal. Nellie Ballard, born in Rockville in 1931, explained. "Well, people gathered Brigham tea. You've heard of Brigham tea. We found that on the hills, just on the hills. Yes, a lot of people hunted for Brigham tea and [would] make a tea out of it! . . . We used it as a medicinal-type thing. Oh, you know, stomach problems or things like that . . . Didn't know what else to do, you drank Brigham tea, I guess." Others, like Yvonne Hoff's family, simply enjoyed drinking it. "We used to drink Brigham Tea. [It grows] everyplace, you know. Cane Beds, Rockville, St. George, Grafton—it's always in the hills. And we'd just brew it up—just boil it, pour it off—it was good stuff. Oh no, we just drank it because it was good. Probably a little sugar, if that. I don't really remember adding anything—it just tasted good the way it was."

Another example of a plant used by both Mormons and Native Americans was the yucca, of which Zion has two species (Nelson 1976). Elva Twitchell detailed:

> There's another herb that we used, the pioneers they say used it a lot when they first come here, they'd dig the root from the "oose," the yucca . . . And cut it up and put it in water and it makes a wonderful soap. It lathers real good. And it was good for your hair . . . But anyway, there was a lot of that used, that's why there isn't so much oose now, yuccas, I should say, growing here. 'Cause we used so much of the root. We'd always try to leave some of the root so that it would keep growing. But I've washed my hair in that a few times; it was nice. I wouldn't go dig one now. It lathers real well.

Her comment in regard to informal "management" of the resource by allowing "some of the roots" to remain, is worth a note. Many writers and western histories have observed that "in the West, most Mormons tie their faith to a culture that, historically, had to subdue the land to survive" (Winters 2003). Brehm and Eisenhauer (2006) comment that, "The arid landscape in the region necessitated the control of nature to make it habitable and fruitful for church members" (p. 397). Others have cited that as a result of their "lack of familiarity as New Englanders and Midwesterners with how arid countries function, the Mormons paid too little attention to the tenuous nature of the natural forces that held Zion together" (Flores 2001, p. 141). However, as Twitchell's and other interviewee comments and anecdotes revealed, some of the pioneers were indeed intimate in their knowledge of the land and expressed concern about their use of resources.

Once pioneers learned about a resource and its use, that use often entailed time-consuming preparation. Another interviewee described the labor-intensive process of making soap that took place during her Zion Canyon childhood. She pointed out how pioneers made use of many resources in a non-wasteful manner.

> They made soap out of . . . the root of trees . . . and they would make lye out of the ashes. And when we made soap, we put it in a big tub and put a fire under it and we'd have to stand and stir that sometimes all day . . . When it was done we could tell by a little taste on the end of your finger. They never wasted anything.

In another conversation, this interviewee described how thread "ends" were saved and re-used in quilting. This pioneer attempt to utilize resources, both natural resources and purchased, to their maximum potential was echoed by other interviewees:

> We'd save all our grease, cooking grease. Never throw away anything like that. And when they'd butcher, they'd take the fat and render it out. And what we don't use for the house we'd use it with lye . . . [for] the soap, or the grease, and cooked it together . . . And you have to stir it a lot if you cooked it, it took a lot of stirring . . . Because we'd have the tub outside with the fire under it. That's the way we did it anyway. Make it in these great big washtubs. And we'd have to sit by it and stir it a lot and get it mixed and so it would heat up all the fat.

While many have emphasized the impact pioneers made on the land, it is worth considering how they also practiced a philosophy of "reuse" long before the modern-day recycling of resources was initiated. Although these habits certainly began out of necessity, this is also a way of life several interviewees proudly recalled as much as eight decades later.

The use of certain natural resources slowed as the division of labor changed. The treatment of mild to moderate health problems, for example, was once primarily a task associated with women. Interviewees who discussed using plants for medicinal purposes did so mostly in relation to their mothers. However, these second and third generation pioneers lived in a transitional time when traditional plant uses were being replaced by "modern" medicine as evidenced by the following quote:

> We had a midwife in Rockville that took care of sickness . . . And, oh, yes, she took care of everything. Right after McIntyre came to Hurricane, he was our doctor for years, and he said that this Becky Dennett, she was the midwife, he said that she taught him a lot of things. He just started here. This is where he come after he got out of school and residency . . . And he said Becky taught him a lot of things he didn't know. Of course, she used a lot of herbs.

Hall's *History of Rockville* (1999) mentions the common use of many medicinal plants by the pioneers including sweet balsam in homemade cough medicine. In addition, he describes Brigham tea used as a treatment for a variety of maladies and oakleaf sumac [once called "squawbush"] tea for canker sore relief, as does Larsen (2004). A Pioneer Voices interviewee described additional medicinal plant uses:

> You may not believe this, but we used to use aspen bark, make a tea out of that, and, for what I don't have the slightest idea now . . . It was so bitter that I tasted it a time or two. I don't know how anybody could drink that stuff . . . But I think my mother's favorite medicinal plant was what we call sweet balsam, and I remember one time, the doctor, I can't remember which doctor, recommended that . . . mother get that and make a tea out of it . . . There's a little place

in Zion, a branch of Oak Creek, a little gully, it's where the upper residents are [today] . . . the name of that gully was Balsam Holler, and there used to be a lot of it growing there. We'd go and gather it. Mother'd make a tea out of it. I don't know if that was supposed to help you get over colds or the flu or that kind of stuff. I'd sometimes pull a leaf off and chew it. It's, oh, slightly pungent. It's waxy when you chew it; your teeth end up kind of gummy. But it kinda has a good taste. You chew it and suck air into it. . . . it's like a mint, a very distinctive flavor. And I think that my parents used more of that than any other native plant . . . for medicinal purposes. Some of the old timers used to make their own salve and they use[d] a combination of mutton tallow and pine gum, sticky pine gum. They'd flavor it up with a number of other things.

J. L. Crawford noted using sap from the pine tree as a child for recreational purposes:

We use[d] to get a Bull Durham sack and fill it up and we always had a supply of that. When I was a kid, most of us my age would go around, if we found a good pine gum tree, we'd keep going back to that tree. We'd get it in those clear little globules, amber colored, and we'd fill our little sack with it. We'd always have a chew of pine gum. I've heard of people chewing gum off the squawbush, but I could never gather enough of that . . . But I heard of people that did. They'd go into a room and everybody would know it. Because it has such an aromatic scent to it. And, to me, I always liked the smell of that, that squawbush and other people call it skunkbush. And to me it is a very pleasant odor.

Yvonne Hoff, born in 1929, whose family was one of the last to live in the town of Grafton before it was abandoned, also lived in Rockville in the 1930s. She shared stories about using sap as chewing gum, and as a unique car repair material. "The sap on the pine trees. We used to chew it. My dad—when we'd go on a trip—we'd chew pine sap and if the car sprung a leak or anything we'd use that to plug the leak! There were a lot of radiators that were plugged up with pine gum . . . it tasted pretty good, I thought. It was really hard and crunchy and crumbly when you first get it off the tree. We used to go collect it off the trees . . . you just keep chewing and chewing and pretty soon it gets just like regular gum."

Hoff also described the ritual of collecting pine nuts from the piñon pine with her family as did other interviewees. These nuts have been collected for centuries and with their high caloric content were an important staple food for early Native Americans throughout the Great Basin (Rhode, 2002 pp. 35–37). Hoff explained how Zion pioneer families gathered and prepared the nuts. "Oh, that was another family outing. We used to go pine nut hunting . . . the whole family . . . we just ate 'em, oh yes! We roasted them in the oven in a shallow pan. Just kind of roasted them a bit . . ."

Wood from local trees, including the pines, was a pioneer necessity for heating and cooking. J. L. Crawford provided interesting observations about the possible effects that harvesting may have had on the local Fremont cottonwood population, a species that resource management in Zion National Park still struggles to re-establish along the banks of the Virgin River today:

I'm amazed there are any [cottonwoods] left, when you consider how many were cut down in pioneer times. And when you look at pictures of the river, you see such a wide flood plain, some places you can't see any cottonwoods. But up where we lived, there was always cottonwoods along the sides of streams and along the river, and in all stages of growth. And I can remember in the spring, we'd get up in the morning and of course we were in that narrow canyon and it was kind of late when the sun would come up. From our house, we'd look over towards Bridge Mountain. Sometimes it would be hard to see it because of the amount of cotton flying in the breeze from the cottonwoods growing along Oak Creek and along the river too. And of course, people, especially my Uncle John Crawford and his family, had several boys in the family. In the winter time they'd cut those cottonwoods and saw . . . they had a Model-T Ford car. They'd hook a pulley onto the rear wheel and use that to power a buzz saw. And they would saw up huge piles of that cottonwood and have big pyramids of it. And of course, they did it for themselves, all members of the family and my grand-mother's home and they'd have a wood shed. And then they'd spend days and days splitting the wood, stacking it for winter use. This would be . . . well, I don't mean just for winter use, for summer! They'd split it when it was still green. If you wait until it's dry, forget it. Then it just doesn't split. Then that would be actually their summer supply because the cottonwood burns clean . . . it doesn't last long. But it does make a hot fire without any dirty mess like . . . it doesn't gum up your stove like pine would. But that isn't the only kind of wood . . . we used the juniper a lot for the cook stove. We didn't use it for open fireplaces because it pops those embers so much. But the cottonwoods were used most for firewood in my time . . . or, the building of fences. I guess the greatest use my father made of the cottonwood is to build dams in the river because they constantly had to build a dam for his ditch. It would wash out maybe three times every summer and he'd have to go rebuild it. What he'd have to do is go chop a cottonwood down and drag it . . . maybe two or three of them . . . and drag it into the river, lodge other brush against it for their diversion dams. So a lot of the cottonwoods were used for that. In the olden days many houses were built out of the logs of cottonwoods. They were used extensively. That's why I say it's a wonder there are any cottonwoods left. And if you look at some of the old pictures you can find, you'll see pictures of cottonwoods, looks like somebody spilled a box of toothpicks. I'm sure what happened . . . they chopped these trees down and they let the horses peel the bark off. Horses love the bark of trees, and they would peel at least off the smaller limbs. And after that, in the spring or whenever, they'd use what's left in building fences, pigpens; use it for firewood . . . a number of uses.

DELLA HIGLEY, BORN 1914

Pioneer Della Higley also mentioned her family using the wood of cottonwood trees, but she noted, "My grandfather would cut limbs off of the trees and plant them along the river. And in a few years he could cut them down to use for wood." This again demonstrated that the ideas of natural resource management and renewable resources were not unknown to the early pioneers, in spite of the fact that the canyon's population was sparse and resources might have seemed deceivingly limitless at that time.

Although the oaks of southern Utah are low and shrubby compared to eastern and northern species, the pioneers harvested them for a specific use. One of Hall's (1999) interviewees related details about using oak for fencing in the greater Zion area:

> There was a field of thirty acres that required two miles of fence, fit to stop a pig. Our three or four old sows and their families ranged over the hills feeding on acorns that dropped from oak trees. Their preference though, was to burrow through the fence and root for potatoes. The best oaks for fencing grew in little swales and fertile flats. They needed to be at least fourteen feet tall, three to four inches in diameter at the base and to have grown in close proximity to one another so there would be few side-branches. The larger of these were cut into seven-foot-length posts, which were then set four feet apart and buried two feet into the ground. Smaller, more supple poles were woven basket-style from post to post up to height of about four and one-half feet (p. 30).

Pioneer Voices interviewee David Terry also recalled using "cedar" [Utah and Rocky Mountain juniper] and pine for firewood. He described, "We used to take the wagon and go out on this, what they call the South Mountain and right about there and got harvest of dead trees for their 'winter supply' . . . You go up the mountain into Grafton . . . You get up at 5:00 in the morning and hook the team up. Go out there and load it up and come back in about dark." Hall (1999) also noted use of juniper bark as an irrigation ditch lining which probably slowed erosion of the freshly-dug banks (p. 37).

In addition to trees used for survival-related purposes, people also often put up Christmas trees over the holidays as J. L. Crawford explained:

We'd just go up in the hills right there at Oak Creek and chop down . . . a piñon pine, [or] sometimes what we'd call a little red Cedar. Which is the Rocky Mountain juniper. You go far enough up Oak Creek you can find the Rocky Mountain juniper and they're a pretty tree when they are young. A lot nicer looking tree than a Utah juniper . . . We'd decorate them with popcorn . . . chains . . . popcorn balls . . . We'd make paper chains, yes. And a few times I remember, when I was a kid . . . We'd get a big [tree] and put it in the church. And have a town party, a Ward Christmas tree and Santa Claus. You know make a community thing out of it. But as for everybody using a tree I couldn't say how much of it . . . but in my opinion, I guess about everybody did.

As they took down trees, Terry also noted that sometimes pioneers also planted them. "Big trees they planted, grew over [and] shaded the entire street [in Rockville]." This past still mixes with the present-day in Southern Utah. Some of the Pioneer Voices interviewees still live along that same tree-canopied Rockville street today. Exotic fruit trees from apples to pears and plums, remnants of long-gone pioneer orchards, are scattered throughout South and Watchman Campgrounds in contemporary Zion National Park.

Not all of the exotic plants brought to Utah, however, proved as benign as Rockville's street trees. Tamarisk, or salt cedar, has become an invasive pest species in many riparian areas including Zion National Park where there have been eradication programs implemented. J. L. Crawford's comments helped to demonstrate the rapid spread of the species around Zion:

When I was a kid, I remember one [Tamarisk] tree, or a big bush. I don't know, it might have been 15 feet high. That's the only one I can remember. I can remember people talking about "tamarack." People still do call it that which is erroneous. And it was a long time before I heard the name tamarisk, or the scientific name *Tamarix*. But there was one bush that grew right near my granddad's old blacksmith's shop. I say my granddad . . . he was dead before I was

AUSTEN EXCELL, BORN 1919

born, so that shop actually belonged to my uncle and, well, my dad . . . the whole neighborhood actually. And to me that [plant] was kind of a novelty. Because to me it was so different. Leaves . . . looked a little like a cedar tree or pine or something. And I don't remember when . . . I was aware the darn stuff had taken over the country . . . I guess by the time I was grown and became a ranger in the park, it had just about lined the river all the way along. But . . . into the 30's. Back in the early 20's when I can remember that one bush, I couldn't say that was the only one in the area, but it's one I knew about. That's the reason it was somewhat of a novelty. Boy, how the stuff has taken over since then and become such a pest.

Crawford's sister affirmed, "I don't think [tamarisk] grew up even as far as Rockville when I was a kid. It mighta done because we didn't get down that way that often, I don't remember it. We didn't have it up here. No we had mostly box elder and ash and things they have up here now. A lot of water willow which you hardly see anymore. They grew along the banks of the river and irrigation ditches."

Crawford noted several other changes in Zion plant communities that he has witnessed over his lifetime:

And the sad thing about it is some of the old native plants have been crowded out by exotics. You don't see much Indian ricegrass anymore. You see cheatgrass and foxtail, and puncture weed. . . . and that's another pest that I didn't know as a kid. It just wasn't there. But in the 1930s it was introduced somehow and it has taken over. It is a real, real pest. Another plant that has taken over is a mustard, a purple mustard. *Chorispora* is the only name I know. I don't know the common name for it, and it's kind of a foul smelling plant. I didn't ever see that plant when I was a kid. And now there's fields of it . . . To me, it's an undesirable plant.

Ailanthus [Tree of Heaven] is another exotic plant species of Asian origin that became fairly common in the canyon around the beginning of the twentieth century as reported by pioneers. This tree became part of a small furniture industry in the Rockville area as described by Austen Excell, "That was a tree that was brought into the country in the early days of Zion to build chairs . . . brought 'em in here because the tree was easy to work with, grew tall and straight and when it dried it was very hard, but it was very soft when it was alive . . . it was a wonderful tree for chair-making because you could bend it and it would stay bent and when it dried it was very hard . . . They made all kinds, dining room chairs, rocking chairs, almost any kind, with rawhide bottoms . . . from hides. [The chairs] last forever."

Mormon settlers harvested native and naturalized wild plants either out of necessity or to supplement their lives. They became knowledgeable about the native plant life around them to the extent that it was useful to them, from medicine and salves to dietary additions or as animal feed. They were also dependent on plant materials for their homes, their furnishings, their heat, and their fencing. As noted from the interviews, pioneers used these natural resources as needed, sometimes being selective and making an attempt at resource management, and other times with the assumption that the resource would replenish itself. The transition that occurred with the establishment of the park, changes in the local economy and workforce, and the development of nearby Hurricane and St. George all impacted the movement away from the use of these plants. Many of these changes happened during the time Pioneer Voices interviewees grew up in the canyon. Their memories today, from poultices to pine sap gum and from piñon nut collection to stewed greens remain an important part of their pioneer heritage.

Contemporary Utah is again in a time of transition. The habitat of many of the species interviewees discussed, from Sego lilies to piñon pine and from yucca to Mormon tea, is currently subject to development and habitat destruction. Many native animal species depend on these plants from pollinators like the yucca moth to foragers like mule deer. Protection of these plant species and their habitats helps to preserve the ecosystem and its biodiversity as well as the heritage of the Zion pioneers and those who came before.

ALMA COX, BORN 1919

Zion Pioneers and Native Animals

ZION CANYON TODAY teems with mule deer, ground squirrels, wild turkeys, porcupines and other animals that survive successfully in the presence of people. More furtive inhabitants such as mountain lions, elk, bear and bighorn sheep, which require large ranges, are present, but seldom seen. Other species, like wolves, have been extirpated and they remain controversial throughout the western United States as possible candidates for re-introduction. To what extent are modern attitudes about wildlife in the West affected by the past? The pioneers of Zion Canyon saw animals like these that surrounded them in the early twentieth century primarily from three vantage points: as potential game or livelihood, as "nuisances" to their domestic animals and crops, or as danger to their own lives. Victor Hall (1999) confirmed that wild animals were viewed as a threat to crops and to farm animals. Controlling them could also be made into a "game" (p. 19) as one of his interviewees explained:

> It was the custom to have competitive scalp hunts to keep predatory pests in check. Two sides were formed with a captain for each side; a time period of several weeks was set. Gophers were the standard unit of measurement. One gopher equaled four mice or chipmunks. One gray squirrel equaled two gophers; raccoons and foxes equaled ten; coyotes equaled twelve, and cougars, twenty-five. The contests were very interesting and intense; the losing side feted the other to a dance or a picnic (p. 19).

Alma Cox, born in Rockville in 1919, described more about these "scalp hunts":

> We had, at one time, a scalp hunt. A scalp hunt, that was to get rid of the mice and the rats and the squirrels and things that were detrimental to our raising crops and nuts and things like that. And a mouse might be one point and a rat two and then gophers two and squirrels, maybe squirrels being 25 or something

cuz they're bad ones and the east end of the town would be against the west end of the town and the losers would have to furnish a feast, a dinner you know, for the rest of 'em and then dance and that. That was an interesting project . . . and it was the tails that we'd keep to . . . turn them in so that they'd prove that you had a mouse or a rat or a gopher or a squirrel or whatever you know.

Some pioneers also earned money from trapping game as Elva Twitchell related:

My father used to trap some of these smaller animals for their pelts. And that was the money he had during the winter. Fox and raccoon and once in a while a coyote, a lotta bobcat. They'd come down into the yard at night, take our chickens if we didn't take care of them.

Her brother J. L. Crawford affirmed:

Maybe I should tell you that my Dad used to trap animals quite a lot. My mother told me fairly late in her life that there was one or two winters when the kids were growing up . . . when the family was young, that we might have gone hungry during the winter had Dad not trapped and sold furs. And I have somewhere a picture floating around. Where my dad has a bunch of skins on a wall probably on the side of his granary. And the animals that he would trap would be foxes, raccoons, [and] ringtail cats. And once in a while . . . Bobcats . . . once in a while a coyote. And a lot of skunks. Dad could skin a skunk without getting a scent on him. He had to ship those specially . . . he had to seal 'em in a metal can. He had to take one of those molasses cans and put a lid on it . . . that was the regulation, I think. Shipped them in the mail you . . . couldn't just wrap them in cardboard or paper. But, he'd send them off to these fur companies. And get a little check back from them.

The interviewer questioned Crawford as to whether beavers had been trapped as well. Beavers are sometimes seen in the Virgin River today where signs of their chewing on cottonwood trees also reveal patterns of their recent presence in the canyon.

Beavers . . . not in my lifetime. And I don't think I was aware that there were ever beavers there until I came home from the war and the people started talking about bank beavers and I said, "What are bank beavers?" They'd say, "They are beavers that live in the bank instead of building dams." Well, then going up Zion Canyon I could see trees . . . they'd [been] working on the cottonwood trees . . . they'd cut a few of them down. But there would be no dams except a time or two they'd start to [build one]. I think the only place I know in Zion where the beavers were building a dam was on this Weeping Rock Creek right below the bridge, between there and the river, they built a dam . . . I think during the 1970s, there was still a little dam there between the bridge and the river. Where Weeping Rock Creek comes out. But I think the beavers got smart and knew that they couldn't build a dam and make it stay in the river. The story is that during the war, beavers had come up the Virgin River from the Colorado. And according to . . . I guess the naturalist was Russell Grater. He told me that, yes, the beavers have always been along the Colorado River. And they'd become a different subspecies because of having to develop different habits. And that they'd probably come up the Virgin River and got into Zion Canyon again and they assume they were there back in [early] pioneer days. But for some reason had disappeared. And I haven't found in the history where they were ever trapping them in the Zion area. And . . . then you hear names of places like Otter Creek, which is not in Zion of course, but people, or historians say there were otters along the Virgin River back in pioneer days, but never in my lifetime. My dad never caught an otter. I remember he used to talk about otters and fishers [and] martins, and they just didn't exist in my lifetime.

The children of the early Zion pioneers were witnesses to changes in patterns of animal populations that occurred throughout their lifetimes. Declines among some Utah

BARBARA BELL, BORN 1918

species have occurred for various reasons, for example, human predation as evidenced by the extirpation of the wolf and the decline of species such as the rattlesnake and prairie dog. Diseases from domestic livestock probably contributed to some declines, for example, the extirpation in some places of bighorn sheep. Toweill (2003) notes that "many herds have experienced a dramatic die-off following exposure to bacterial agents carried by apparently healthy domestic sheep" (p. 39). Habitat destruction and fragmentation have also impacted sheep as well as desert tortoise and black bear populations. On the other hand, a few species, such as mule deer and coyotes, seem to have exploded since Spanish explorers Dominguez and Escalante explored Utah in 1776. The destruction of predator species may have facilitated the rise of deer and coyote populations, and the human "management" of the mule deer for hunting may be another contributing factor. Today, most visitors to Zion National Park have an excellent chance of seeing at least a few deer during their vacation. J. L. Crawford noted that in his youth, it was quite a different story:

> I was nine years old before I saw a deer, and growing up in Zion Canyon—that sounds strange. But I suppose in those early days, if they had game laws, they weren't enforced. And there was a lot of poaching going on, so there just weren't many deer around the country. And after that first one I saw, seemed like they just ballooned and they became very common and before we left Oak Creek, there were big herds of them and they'd come into our orchards at night and raise heck with the fruit, all they could reach. These white cling peaches, they like those, you know, get [ripe] about almost deer season time. They'd be in there standing on their hind legs, pick those peaches . . . But the deer population increased faster than people could poach them out.

His sister confirmed, "When I was small, I didn't see any. I remember my father got a deer clear up on the Sand Bench, before it was a park. And he got a deer and that was the only deer I remember until after I was grown up."

Lorna (Jolley) Kesterson mentioned her father, Zion Chief Ranger Donal Jolley, who patrolled for poachers along the park borders in the 1920s. "Dad did a lot of horseback riding during like hunting season. He had to ride the boundaries because some of the deer hunters always poached in the park."

In the 1920s and 1930s, other animals were hunted besides deer:

Chief Ranger Donal Jolley, Zion National Park, 1920s.

Well, we used deer. We used to go hunting, you know, just when we needed the meat. We didn't go for the hunt. We went when we needed the meat. We used to go and we'd get deer every year, and cottontail, a course that'un didn't amount to too much! But cottontails is good to eat! They're good meat . . . One time we kids got some cottontails when we was having a dinner and we got some squirrels that same day and we thought, "why don't we take some of this squirrel meat home and take it and put it in with the cottontail meat." And we did and we thought we'd fool the people who was at the dinner, you know, and they was a eatin' away and enjoying the meat and we could tell the difference, because, well we could tell the difference between the two kinds of meat, and they got that squirrel meat, and [said], "Oh, why this is sure good." Shoot, we were there grinnin' because we thought, "Well, isn't that something, pulling a trick like that on 'em." We just couldn't stand it any longer, we had to get a piece of squirrel meat . . . and see how it tasted like and it was good too! Porkypine meat is not too good, it's kinda bad and all that . . . a course it'd save your life a lotta times . . . cuz they were around . . . if you ever get lost and you're starving, well, hunt a porkypine. You can save your life.

Della Higley also recalled sampling "new" tastes as a child in the 1930s. "Well, we . . . we had lots of wild rabbits and squirrels and . . . us kids decided once we wanted to know what a squirrel tasted like so the boys got the squirrel and we girls cooked it on a campfire. I don't remember exactly what it tasted like, but that's the only one we ever had."

Larger predators of the Zion area, however, were not to be taken so lightly. Mountain lions, bears and wolves were unusual sightings even in pioneer times, although Hall (1999) notes that they were more common then than they are today (p. 80). When these large carnivores were sighted or discussed, they were often the subject of worry among pioneers who feared their ability to attack domestic animals or humans. Despite the fearsome reputation of these wild animals, few Pioneer Voices interviewees confirmed actually having seen large carnivores, even those who spent much of their childhood outdoors. Attacks by bears and mountain lions were rare, but reported. Most "encounters" resembled these descriptions from J. L. Crawford:

I never did see a mountain lion or hear much about them; it was quite a novelty when an uncle of mine . . . and another fella killed a cougar up on top of the mountain and got it down and showed it off. Then I heard stories about getting a cougar once in a while, but that was rare. While we still lived at Oak Creek I remember, one time a cougar went across our field and, I supposed my mother and sister almost encountered that cougar . . . We had a garden about where the ranger dormitory is now . . . my mother and one of my sisters went into the garden; I guess they were getting some onions, radishes, and stuff like that, that they were going to have for an evening meal. It was just getting dark and my father was up the canyon for some reason. [There] used to be a lot of quail around the area. Suddenly they heard this flock of quail fly up from a little thicket that was near the garden and they commented there, "I guess dad's coming down the canyon" but he didn't show up and he came in later and they said, "We thought you were going to meet us at the garden." The next day they discovered that a cougar had walked right past the garden where they were. So they figured that then the cougar had disturbed the quail. As for other predators, dad talk[ed] about wolves being very rare . . . I'm sure my brother and I heard a wolf howl one time and don't know how old I was then, maybe nine or eleven. We'd gone to a chicken coop which is at the upper end of the field which would be over that way from the . . . administration building. So we walked . . . a little trail . . . on the side of the orchard between the orchard and the alfalfa field. And we were walking from that and we could hear some yelling up the canyon, up Oak Creek Canyon and we wondered, is somebody up there singing, sounded kinda [like a] deep voice. And we got to the house and said, "Who's up Oak Creek?" They could be yelling or singing or something . . . And we forgot about it till years later when I heard a wolf howl. . . . I asked mother, of course. Dad was dead by then . . . She said, "Yeah we knew it was howling there, but we weren't about to tell you kids. . . afraid it would scare you and you [would] never get out of the house alone."

Not all encounters were harmless, however, with Hall (1999) reporting a bear attack near what is now the Kolob Terrace Road that nearly ended in the death of a man. He also related (p. 105) this confrontation between one pioneer and a wolf over livestock, by Crystal Ranch:

He arrived at the scene just in time to stop a wolf from killing some sheep. He carried a gun for such emergencies, but not this day; it was back at the sheep-wagon. The wolf stood its ground. It wasn't sure about attacking this intruder, but it was loath to give up a fine mutton dinner. Finally, Vern picked up a couple of rocks and threw one. It struck a tree just to the side of the wolf's head. As the wolf jerked its head sideways in response to the noise, Vern threw again. This time he scored and the bruised wolf withdrew. This ended Vern's fear of wild animals.

Austen Excell remembered seeing a wolf at least two times on the east side of Zion. Since Excell did not move to the Canyon until 1930 with his family, the sighting occurred

EVELYN BLEAK, BORN 1913

sometime after that date. J. L. Crawford has a special interest in and knowledge about the subject of wolves, fueled by the fact that he is a naturalist and former ranger. He noted during his interview that:

> The last authentic record of wolves in the area [was] 1936. A friend of mine, Harmon Reusch, said that he and Adrian Dennett [were going] out "in the Sands"... Dennetts had a ranch and that was ... where, if you go up Pahrunaweep just on top of the mountains there off Shune's Creek in that area . . . they call the Sands . . . And the Dennetts had a ranch up there in the thirties. And [they] were up there, said they shot at a couple of wolves and missed them of course. But Cliff Presnall, first permanent naturalist that Zion had, did a book [and] he said the last record of wolves were that same year, 1936, when two of them were trapped or killed near Short Creek. They were in the area that late.

While wolves were hunted to near extinction in the western states, coyotes, although reviled by many, have been more successful at evading human campaigns to eradicate them. Their keen sense of survival earned them the attention and respect of Native Americans in the Zion area, and nearby Mt. Kinesava takes its name from their spirit. Woodbury (1997) notes "*Kai-ne-sava* was fond of playing pranks" (p. 113). While coyotes were considered nuisances and were hunted and trapped by early Zion settlers, nonetheless, the pioneers were not entirely without a nostalgic Western view of the species. One Zion pioneer recounted:

> We older boys drove the cattle to an enclosure for the night then pushed our way through the high sagebrush guided by the campfire the folks had going. Most years though, I remained at the ranch until late in the fall to look after interests generally and look for stray cattle to take down later. When I did make the journey home, I would be serenaded from Crystal to clear down below the Caves by coyotes who seemed to have gathered in packs for that purpose. Maybe they were just lonesome and wanted to go on home with me (Hall 1999, p. 81).

Bighorn sheep also have an interesting history in Zion National Park. Once they were very common in parts of the West. The Dominguez and Escalante diaries from the 1776 expedition noted, "Wild sheep breed . . . in such abundance that the tracks look like those of great droves of tame sheep" (Warner 1995, p. 123). Bighorn sheep were locally extirpated in several places including Zion in the twentieth century. In the park, however, they were re-introduced with some success in the 1970s. An interviewee in Hall (1999) comments that in the pioneer era, "Mountain sheep were quite common. One big fellow was seen leaving the river and going to the hills past the Crank fields. Dave Lemmon who lived nearby grabbed his gun and soon bagged his game. Pa, in telling it, said the buck's horns were as big as a man's leg" (p. 74).

Pioneer Voices interviewee Lorna Jolley (born 1925), daughter of Zion National Park's first chief ranger Donal Jolley, tells a story of having a Bighorn sheep temporarily "quartered" in park housing:

> In Zion we couldn't have anything penned like a dog but we had a lot of deer in the yard and ring-tailed cats and one mountain sheep that took over our whole house inside until finally Dad decided he was too rough. [The sheep] would come in and slide the rug. [My father] finally decided the sheep was too rough for us.

Those who lived in Zion Canyon in the 1930s witnessed the final natural bighorn population in Zion prior to their re-introduction from other western populations in the 1970s. Austen Excell, who moved to Zion as a child noted, "Well, when we first come into Zion [in 1930], there was bighorn sheep here . . . We seen them for a few years and finally they disappeared. We saw [Bighorn] right above the [Zion] tunnel, coming in one time, bighorn sheep there . . . But it wasn't very many years after that they all disappeared . . . something just got rid of them all at once. I don't know whether it was disease or what it was. [We didn't see them . . .] until later on when they did introduce them again."

An interviewee discussed another species that few visitors to Zion see, the nocturnal ringtail cat, a relative of the raccoon:

There'd be ringtail cats once in awhile. There was more of them, I think, than there is now. But the raccoons left for a long time . . . we didn't know of a raccoon here in the country. Now they're thick again . . . they were here years ago . . . [People would] take old clothes and hang them on the corn stalks to keep the raccoons away, 'cause they'd eat it!

She also noted that, "There was a lot of hawks. We had to watch hawks all the time; they were after our chickens. And I remember seeing one eagle when I was a kid and it landed on that hill up there, just before you get to the old visitor center. And there was a big eagle come and landed on that hill and my dad had us go to the window and see it because it was the first eagle we'd ever seen." J. L. Crawford reminisced about how raptors were considered a threat to the pioneer food supply: "We didn't have just hawks. No, in those days, we had chicken hawks. Hawks ate chickens, so they were supposed to be better off dead. So we'd try to kill them. Crows, ravens and owls and snakes were dangerous. They can bite you and kill you, so you were to kill them . . . I guess everybody had guns and they'd try to kill hawks . . ."

Crawford continued on to detail the pioneer aversion to reptiles: "Well of course, we [were] always conscious of snakes. And all snakes were 'bad,' so . . . I remember when we use[d] to kill the gopher snakes even, and, it was a long while before I knew how beneficial they were, and I think we should have known better . . . I wouldn't say a lot, but we had rattlers. We heard about one person in Springdale that was bitten by a rattlesnake when he was young, and he got to be a really big huge person. People thought it was because that poison of that rattlesnake had made him that way. Later on, I knew better. It was because he was a big eater and so he was that way! So they were around and of course we were cautious of them."

The Zion Canyon pioneers shared similar views with other Western settlers and resembled them in attempts to "tame a wilderness" and its animal inhabitants. Animal species were measured by whether they were perceived as a threat to life, crops and livestock, as a "useful" species, or as a "beautiful" species that gave pleasure to people. In examining these historical attitudes and actions of people in regard to the wild animals around them, we can find the roots of some beliefs that still prevail today. By discovering and understanding the origins of these ideas, including misconceptions about predators, we may better ensure that animals and people in the American West can co-exist for the future.

Zion Pioneers, Land Use and the Virgin River

"OVER THE PAST TWO MILLION years the Virgin River has been the key player in Zion Canyon's formation" (Eves 2005, p. 8). In the same way it determined the shape of the canyon, it has also had a profound sculpting effect on the lives of the settlers who lived along its banks and floodplains. At times, it was a placid ribbon of water that children swam in during southern Utah's summer heat. The Virgin River was also where Springdale and Rockville families enjoyed picnic lunches after church, and where pioneer boys caught "suckers" and trout. Occasionally, the river even held a spiritual purpose. Hall (1999) describes a baptism in the Virgin River on March 3, 1906 "as an event that stood out in [one boy's] memory of his Rockville childhood" (p. 101). At other times, the river was a force of destruction to the settlers as it had been to the Paiutes and the Ancestral Puebloans before them. The Virgin wiped away crops, barns and bridges in an instant, taking topsoil, livestock, property, and occasionally, human lives. One interviewee discussed the impact of the river on his life:

> Well, I been fighting the [Virgin] River all my life. Of course, not right now I'm not, haven't got the energy to fight it. But when them big floods would come down, of course we knew this Virgin River was mighty important to us 'cuz it furnished us our drinking water for a long, long time until we got our springs.

And it furnishes us with our irrigatin' water all the time clear up to the present time. But sometimes it'd come down and it'd wash away people's farms, crops and all. I remember it took a lot of our farmland away with the crops already on it. Cane all ready for cutting or harvesting, you know, for making sorghum out of. And we had peas that we took to market . . . but . . . the floods didn't care about what kinds of crops was on 'em. It just took 'em and took 'em away!

J. L. Crawford witnessed flooding, changes in flood plains and the effects of grazing:

I think that the river channel, in some places, might be as much as 20 feet deeper than it was when I was a kid. That would maybe be excessive, and it wouldn't be in all places. Generally, the channel is deeper. It might only be 5 feet deeper in places, but much more . . . There used to be a wider flood plain when you come out of Zion, when you get down to say, Rockville, and Grafton. From the old pictures you see . . . wide flood plains and maybe no vegetation. And I've gone to two or three of these places where those pictures were taken from, and many of them, you can't see the river because of vegetation growing there now . . . the old pioneers probably chopped a lot of the cottonwoods down, but then I'm sure the floods took a lot of them out. You don't see one flood now, where we use to see a dozen maybe, and the reason for that is, when I was a kid there was still thousands of sheep into the watersheds. They say Long Valley, Left Fork of the Virgin, even up on Cedar Mountain maybe, there wouldn't be enough vegetation left there to catch the rain. Every time it rained, we'd have a flood . . . I remember a lot of times we could hear the roar of the river, and we'd rush out and there'd be a flood and here it wasn't even raining at our place, but it was up in the mountains. So, floods were so common back in those days . . . I've seen floods come up and wash out some of the crops . . . I remember one place . . . in the South Campground, where the amphitheater [is now] there's a lower area between there and the river . . . we called that the "Sand Bottom." And my uncle use to grow fields of sorghum cane, maybe corn, and floods used to come up and cover that area . . . I can remember it leveling a field of something there once when I was a kid. But, it may have done it several times. And people in Springdale would have areas down close to the river flooded out by floods . . . we like[d] to have it rain, but then we knew we'd have to rebuild an irrigation dam to get the water back in the ditches every time that would happen. And they were a mixed blessing . . . although they'd take the dam out and maybe before the dam would go . . . the flood would carry enough of the mountain soil down and my father used to be tickled to death when he'd find it had washed out onto his field, because it was richer stuff. And Springdale had some pretty poor soil to begin with. It's right in that Chinle layer, where all that blue clay is in there. We like to get that river sand in there to mix with it and help the crops grow. But it took a lot of work to keep that water coming. 'Course when the flood would come, maybe you'd get a little water from the flood, and then right away it['d] stop because the dam would go.

Alder and Brooks (1996) provide support for Crawford's statement about the amount of livestock in the region. They note that by 1900 there may have been nearly 15,000 sheep and 7,000 cattle in Washington County alone (p. 283).

Hall (1999) noted that calamities such as soil erosion that destroyed half of the arable land available to the upper Virgin settlements, and droughts were common problems (p. 15). Ecological issues from overgrazing to erosion and flooding were not limited to the Zion Canyon area. Flores (2001) writes:

Between 1928 and 1930, sixteen Utah counties suffered such devastating floods that Governor George Dern appointed a Flood Commission to study the causes of a phenomenon that had been unknown to the early settlers. After two years of study, the commission concluded that the mountain topography of Utah was incapable of absorbing the kinds of heavy summer rains the region had been

Nora Flanigan Bradshaw, born 1908

experiencing with the watersheds so depleted from grazing, logging, and a rash of fires associated with the highly flammable exotic, cheatgrass (p. 139).

Another Pioneer Voices interviewee discussed floods on land that is now a part of Zion National Park:

I remember floods. We had a lotta floods down that Oak Creek wash. Sometimes I've seen as many as five streams come off those mountains up there, in the head of the canyon and down Balsam Holler . . . there just up above the [park] housing. And then the canyon next to it; there'd be some big floods come outa there . . . [The Virgin] would flood a lot. We had a lot of summer storms. That was through July and August, we'd have so much rain. Oh, yes, I remember the floods . . . if it got stormy, cloudy even, up the canyon, we stayed away from the river . . . It did [affect the crops] because it washed the dams out of the river then our ditches would be dry until they put in a new dam. It was washing away the dams and then we couldn't water the fields.

One interviewee told the following story. "My mother talked about—when we lived in Grafton—standing on that little swinging bridge, watching a flood go down. It was trees and boulders, and she said that if there'd been an animal or a person in there they would not have survived. It was just awful. And I guess that's one reason that Grafton just became a ghost town." Losses due to flooding of property, crops and livestock were not uncommon. "Ah, every once in awhile the river would take up people's crops. But one time it flooded, and it was so heavy that my Uncle Freeborn—had his barn down by the river so that the horses and the animals could get water without him having to carry it—and it took out his barn and all of his animals. It was what we called 'The Hundred-Year Floods' because they really had some big ones in those days."

Although many pioneers descended directly from those sent to southern Utah on the "Cotton Mission," cotton did not take hold in Zion Canyon. However, other agricultural efforts did, which allowed settlers to survive, barter and sell food products.

Despite the scarcity of water in many years, the pioneers did grow successful crops ranging from wheat to sorghum to fruit. The yield was bountiful enough to support some export. The pioneers tell the agricultural story in their own words, "It was nice. Raised a lot of fruit. Vegetables. Mother used to can a thousand quarts of peaches a year . . . Oh, I can see apples, pears, plums [and] apricots. One old [apple] tree in the place today . . . it was planted back in my grandfather's day. So that tree is going to be 120 years old. Still has beautiful, big red apples." Another described in detail the agricultural barter system that evolved:

One of the activities in the summer, we dried fruit. We'd have great big sacks of dried fruit. And in the fall, why some of the men would gather up this dried fruit and the sorghum made from the cane, the big cane beds, and they made either sorghum here or molasses. And they'd take a lot of that north anywhere from Panguitch and Cedar on up, maybe as far as Delta. They didn't grow [cane] up there. And we couldn't grow potatoes very well down here. So we'd trade for wheat and potatoes. And whatever we had to trade that they didn't have— they'd trade back and forth. And so we did that a lot while I was growing up. Ah, we grew nearly everything here, but the main things we would dry would be the nectarines, peaches, and apples, apricots. We grew grapes and quince and cherries. And we had, oh, several different varieties of apples and peaches.

The variety of crops that most families grew seemed to provide them with a full table and diverse tastes:

We just had nearly all the vegetables. We had asparagus, peas, corn, and green beans and cabbage, lettuce, radishes . . . And celery. . . . Oh, the bugs get to them bad. After we moved down here [to Rockville] I couldn't raise cabbage. We grew great big heads up there in the park, but after we moved down here it didn't do very well. Parsnips was another one we raised a lot of. We could store them for winter . . . And we raised oh, several different kinds of squash . . . Pumpkins and little heart squashes and crooknecks, hubbards, I can't even remember the names now. All them we raised.

Interviewees explained that peaches were one of the most successful crops in Zion Canyon as evidenced by this description from Nora (Flanigan) Bradshaw, born in 1908 in Springdale, Utah:

> We had peaches, peaches and peaches. When I was a teenager I was working in peaches. In fact, me and my sister-in-law would pack out three ton of peaches a day. We didn't pick them. We had pickers and sorters, and then my sister-in-law and I would just pack them in the boxes. When we first started we wrapped them and placed them in the boxes one-two-three, then one-two, then one-two-three . . . that's how we packed them in those crates. We had about 40 or 60 acres of peaches. Our family put in the orchard. My father [David Flanigan] built the water wheels that took the water out of the Virgin River to water the orchards. I don't think anyone around here ever built one like that. It was big. It would lift water up 50 feet in the air or something like that. Then it ran out into a flume and then watered the trees.

Not all pioneers had Flanigan's ingenuity or his access to water. Hall (1999) notes that dry-farming also was widespread in the early twentieth century, and that it had an effect on the land:

> As indicated earlier, a major reason for selling the Crystal property was to gain necessary capital for dryfarming. Alf, unlike his father, was able to recognize opportunities, to organize resources, and to aggressively pursue a project to bring about its success. There are hints that Kezia had those same traits, and we can suppose that she passed them on to Alf. Dryfarming, raising grain without irrigation at the higher elevations, was discovered to be feasible about 1900 and

VILO DEMILLE, BORN 1915, AND GREAT-GRANDSONS LANCE AND LANDON

soon thousands of acres on Smiths Mesa and on the "Big" and "Little Plains" about ten miles east of Hurricane were under the plow—and more vulnerable to erosion (p. 40).

These natural limits of the land contributed to the time of transition that occurred during the first third of the twentieth century in the lives of the Zion area pioneers. The limits explain, in part, the pattern of earlier Zion canyon settlers who sold their land, some reluctantly, to either the federal government or to non-locals who settled in the canyon. Alder and Brooks (1996) ask, "Why did some people move and others stay? First, the land for farming was limited . . . If families could subsist on such meager plots, they certainly could not divide them among heirs. Second generation sons knew early on that they would have to seek new lands" (p 82). Families with six, seven or eight children were not uncommon. Land parcels were not divisible in that many sub-parcels, and Rockville and Springdale, sandwiched in between the formations of Zion, simply had limited land available for agriculture. In addition to land issues, water in the desert was another challenging and evolving resource issue.

Drinking water came from the Virgin River when the first pioneers settled in Zion Canyon. J. L. Crawford explained, "Drinking water . . . most of the people dipped it out of the river, the Virgin River or out of the irrigation ditches. We were quite fortunate in having a little spring on our property [at Oak Creek]. Beautiful clear cool water, so we had pretty good drinking water most of the time. So we were lucky."

Not only did the river provide drink, but it sometimes provided food as well. Many of the pioneers did not fish in the Virgin River and some children only did so for recreation. However, several interviewees reported eating the fish that they caught in the river. One explained, "My father, I heard him talking to a cousin who was a lady . . . they both said that they thought sucker [from the Virgin River] was a better eating fish than trout, except for the bone . . . They had so many millions of small bones in them that it was miserable to eat them, but they thought it was better tasting meat than trout."

J. L. Crawford summed up best the importance of the Virgin River to the pioneers:

I think maybe the reason my grandfather went up that canyon is the same reason that an uncle of mine gave. I heard him telling this one time, this is Moses Gifford, one of my dad's uncles . . . some of the tourists asked him what on earth inspired or moved the people? What drew them in here? How can they settle here? And one word explained it . . . water. That was that Virgin River that never went completely dry so that was a good endless supply of water and without water you don't grow food or your crops. Without your crops you don't eat, so that was the lifeblood of the area.

In spite of the pioneers' many struggles with the river, the Virgin and its tributaries provided sustenance, irrigation and recreation. One interviewee described:

Quite often we were with our cousins, but if not, just my brothers and sisters. But you know that creek that comes down by the visitor center (Oak Creek). That went through our farm. And so we were always, in the spring of the year, we'd go along that wash, hunt pollywogs, the pollywogs in the pools. We clumb trees, we climbed rocks just all over the area there. I go up there now I think sometimes, "Oh we used to climb on that rock." This one rock, we thought it was so high . . . we'd get up on it and jump off. . . . after I grew up and was back up there I looked at that rock—it's about that high . . . it's flat on top. We thought that was such a feat that we could get up on the back of it and jump off. Yes, once and awhile we would. Get on the buckboard and go up and usually there'd be two families at least that would go up together. I remember once we went up into the Narrows at the end of the road there at the Temple of Sinawava. My father took pictures there. But my folks they all cooked up a big lunch and took it up there and us kids had a ball playing in the river and running up and down the canyon.

All interviewees had childhood memories of the joy of the river, as is evidenced by Nellie Ballard, "Also my girlfriend and I, in the summertime, our mothers would let us go in the ditch that ran around the bottom of that hill. They never seemed to worry about us. I'd be scared to death to let my kids go in the river now! But we used to spend a lot of time in the ditch. With the water in it. And in the river. All of the kids spent their summers in the river. Both in Rockville and Springdale."

Pioneer Voices interviewee Oscar Johnson, born in Springdale in 1932, described attempts to "improve" swimming holes by local children:

Oh, we swam in the river quite often. We found ponds that were anywhere from two or three feet deep to some that we made that were deep as four or five feet. Up in [Pine Creek]. We'd go up there every year usually, where the floods took it out, we'd reset the rocks [and] it would make us a nice pond. There's a natural spillway that used to come down over and [is] still there I'm sure. We'd just go out past that and build a rock dam across . . . that would let the water through okay, but we built it up so the water would go higher and we could swim in it.

Fae (Terry) Jenacaro was born in 1917 in Rockville, daughter of the pioneer family that owned the Rockville Mercantile. Her comments revealed a similar childhood love of the water mixed with a strong image of how flash floods in the Virgin River provided a distinct memory that she has retained for more than eight decades:

Oh [the Virgin River] was a wonderful place. And you know, we used to go down there all the time and just walk and get in it. It was never deep enough that we were in trouble. I can remember walking barefoot on the sand. All the little crusty places where it would overflow and then clay, and it would curl up. We'd go swimming in it all the time, it was just great. And one of the things I remember most about it is when we'd have a flood, it would have just a great smell, with all of the wood coming down and all the wet stuff. And if you've ever smelled it, you'll never forget it . . . I can't even tell you what it is. It's just something in your memory that sticks . . . wet wood . . . It's like nothing else . . . There's a very unique, peculiar, significant odor to a flood.

CLARA COPE, BORN 1925

Memories like these were embedded in the minds of these children of Zion Canyon who carried them across the country and across time. They returned to the Virgin River of their youth in their memories by bringing their grandchildren to swim in the same spots and by holding southern Utah and the whim of a river in their minds and hearts.

Alder and Brooks (1996) note in their thorough *History of Washington County* that the Native Americans who lived in Zion first lived on the river and on the land in a relatively low impact way. This was due to their limited population size, hunting and gathering lifestyle, small-scale agriculture and light use of natural resources (p. 42). Alder and Brooks compare that historic lifestyle to the pioneers of later days who planted and irrigated aggressively, noting, "The land balked at this change. It did not quickly yield to the determination of the newcomers. It fought back with drought. It responded to overgrazing with flooding. The interface was not natural, and both the land and the people sustained injury. That conflict continues to this day" (p. 42).

Washington County [in which much of Zion is located] is projected to be the fastest growing county in the state, with an average annual growth rate of 3.9% (St. George Chamber, 2006). Today, new "pioneers" arrive in Utah from the northern Wasatch Front for the warmer weather, but also from California, Nevada and across the United States. The water and land-use issues are often surprisingly familiar.

Zion Pioneers and the National Park

THE CREATION OF Mukuntuweap National Monument in 1909, which became Zion National Park in 1919 (Crawford 2002, p. 11), greatly impacted the lives of the inhabitants of Zion Canyon in several ways. The influx of tourists changed the local economy, the establishment of the park imposed rules and fees that were new to local residents, and it also led to the buyout of land from some families which extended the boundaries of the park. Transportation and roads to Zion improved, and the journey to and from Hurricane and St. George, Utah, could be made in hours rather than days. The creation of the park paralleled the transition from the agricultural self-sufficiency and barter experienced by first and second generation pioneers to the "modern" labor-force based lifestyles of third generation pioneers and their descendants.

How did those who lived in and around Zion perceive the change in land designation? What happened when the park boundaries were established and when their home place became world-renowned for its scenery? There was sadness among older settlers for a lost way of life, resentment from some about restrictions designed to protect natural resources, and a sense of gladness from others in sharing their "treasures" with visitors from across the world. Looking back, some felt that a land ethic that early settlers possessed had been marginalized in modern times. One feeling most interviewees shared, however, was the sense that the land of Zion and their heritage intertwined with it, greatly shaped their lives.

Della Higley gave insight into the sense of curiosity and wonder many of the children of Zion had about the new park visitors when she said, "They brought them down in buses from Cedar City. They would come to Cedar on the train and then they had buses that . . . would come down every day and let the people down to the Lodge. And there was very few cars in those days, and . . . so when there was a car we always had to run out to see it. And if there was an airplane we'd have to run out to see an airplane." Sometimes the changes meant great excitement, at other times, the change undoubtedly seemed bittersweet as one pioneer explained. "This was home . . . I guess we didn't have too much to do with the outside world but we could see that it was coming to us because of the park. And . . . I guess we just accept[ed] that." That change came, indeed, and it increased at a rapid pace after 1919.

Those whose land was purchased by the United States government had the most intense emotions, as remembered by their descendents. J. L. Crawford summed up the differences between how the early and later generations in Zion Canyon felt about the changes:

> Most of my generation was kind of fed up with trying to make a living on those
> little pieces of land, trying to keep irrigation water in, but once you've lost your

irrigation water, you didn't have a crop, and if you didn't have a crop, you didn't eat . . . So, our father, I'm sure, decided the best thing to do would be to dispose of the land . . . since they had a chance to sell [to the government]. Then [my parents] were aware that it could have been a condemnation had they refused to sell. The government wanted it and they were going to get it one way or another . . . I think we weren't paid enough for it . . . but that was in 1931 right in the middle of the Depression so I guess they were glad to get it. My father just went down canyon a couple of miles and bought another home . . . it was a fairly good feeling. Except for my grandmother, my dad's mother [who had moved here in 1879]. She had raised her family there. She had seen it go from a wild canyon to a beautiful ranch. She had a nice home. She'd raised her family there and she was bitter. [She said] "Why don't they just knock me in the head and leave me here."

Crawford's sister Elva Twitchell related more details about this poignant contrast between generations:

I think they were glad of [the new national park], until they come down and started taking our farms. I think they were glad to have the park here. It brought people in and that meant more money, more work for the people here. So I think they were very glad to have it. I remember there was sure a big celebration when they opened it. I remember them cutting the ribbon . . . The Church President, the Governor of the state, there was a lot of dignitaries here. And one time, President Harding . . . came to Zion.

She also related the tale of her father's garden that he left behind when he sold his land to help create Zion National Park:

We had a big garden. A big orchard and my father raised watermelon. He sold watermelon. People clear down to St. George come up for some of his melon. He

Zion National Park's original headquarters, built in 1923–24.

was a natural horticulturist. He had everything in his orchard. He had peaches ripen from May until November, except two weeks during July, and . . . he had just found peaches he thought would ripen during that time and was going to start them when we had to move out. Oh, it was hard to move out. They had to chop down all the orchards . . . they added to the park later so Watchman Campground and all that area was taken in later, and they had them leave the orchards. He took the pecan trees and had chairs made. He made some of them. It was good hardwood. So a lot of our chairs were made from the pecan trees they cut down there. Let's see. He died when he was 62 and we were only here [in town] two or three years when he died. So he was in his late 50s when he moved out.

Twitchell was asked in an interview if she thought people felt differently about the park during this period and she responded:

I don't know. It's different people here now. I don't know how they feel about it. I hated to leave the park, but I didn't . . . I don't remember feeling really bad about it. Except for, I did in this way: I hated to see these older people move. Like grandmother and all her family. The boys were all too old to go out and start over again. And when they had to do it, it was hard. 'Cause they was all situated so that they were getting along you know and then they had to start over and plant orchards and everything, unless they could buy an orchard. My father did . . . him and his brother bought this area from Dennis's fence down through the Driftwood [Lodge]. There was a big orchard there, in the Driftwood. My father took that part and Uncle Jim took this part over here . . . I think we felt alright about the land. I did hate to see them buy the second time because they'd run it down so far. And then there was talk about them buying the whole town of Springdale. Well, I don't think it went very far. In the first place the government, I don't think, wanted to put out that money. And they'd gone far enough when they got down to the line that it's in now. But when they first started the park I think everybody was happy to see it come. It had been a monument for a long while, about nine, ten years. So I think we were all glad to see the park come along because it brought livelihood for the people that lived here. And then they started building roads and that brought more work.

One interviewee, whose family operated a restaurant in 1930s Zion Canyon added, "Well, we liked [the national park]. We were always business-oriented, and that was our source of business." Another described,

Well, I think the [people in Zion Canyon]—they felt good about the park being here, and they felt good when the tunnel was built, I think, because they knew it would be so much easier to get up on the mountain. But they, I'm sure, didn't want to lose their homes. Because they had built this land up from the time that it was a wild country until they were sixty and seventy years old and then to have to move out was a very, very big hardship . . . [the] land they sold, they didn't, weren't able to sell it for enough to really replace it. Well . . . I don't know how my folks felt about it. I know that they didn't want to move away from here because they loved the land so much. So all but one of their brothers, they settled here in Springdale and they didn't want to leave . . . I think about the park—that they felt like my grandmother said, "Why couldn't they let me stay in my home until I died?" And she was eighty-six at the time.

As in most national park gateway communities, there have been mixed feelings through the decades in Zion Canyon about the changes in lifestyle and access related to the park. For example, one interviewee reflected on the change to a shuttle bus system in Zion National Park, initiated in 2000, which restricts access to part of the park by public vehicle during the busiest times of the year. While the idea was controversial when proposed, most community residents seem to support it today. Nonetheless, there are those who grew up in Depression-era Zion Canyon who continue to feel resistance to change. One interviewee commented:

> Well, I don't know how everybody else feels today. I feel that I've lost a lot. You can't go into the park now during the summer and just enjoy a ride to the end of the road and back like we used to do. And I just, I think it's quite a bit different . . . I know. I know. I don't know how they feel about it, but as we've ridden through the park, we go up in the fall after the shuttles, you see a lot of those flat spaces that there is nothing on there not even trees, just weeds. Why can't they clear them off and make big parking areas for people? So they could enjoy it. I don't go to the park much anymore. That's the difference. It's changed a lot.

This evidenced that not all local residents have embraced the changes that have occurred since the land of Zion moved from private place to public space. However, this reflected a minority viewpoint overall. Most interviewees agreed that the shift was both inevitable as well as an opportunity for the country as a whole. Yvonne Hoff explained what she and her family felt was gained in the process, personally, and for all those who visited Zion:

> We thought of [Zion] as a very important park—we were so glad it was there. We loved that park. Loved to go camping and hiking and . . . that was our favor-

ite outing. Well, I think we realized how important that was; I mean country-wise . . . that is . . . was such a marvelous thing, such a wonderful thing. I think it's just wonderful that they had the foresight to set aside that park so that it didn't get overgrown with people, and houses, and towns and things. And . . . thank goodness for it! Can you imagine what that park would have been like if they hadn't made it a park. Yeah. Well . . . my world was pretty small, as a matter of fact, at the time—and that was part of my world, a very important part. I think it would have been terrible not to have that—I can't imagine not having had Zion.

Several of the pioneer children remembered camping and family trips in the early days of Zion National Park:

I remember camping in the park. We camped up in what is the Grotto now, but it was a campground—long time ago. And we always camped at the upper end where there's a side stream that comes down out of a little side canyon. And we used to hike up that—it was so pretty and it was so quiet. Weren't too many people there camping then, but we really enjoyed camping . . . They used to block up the river—the main river—you know just above the swinging bridge. Another swinging bridge—I used to have nightmares about swinging bridges! Until I was grown up. I never hit the water, but I always fell off. But they used to block the river so it made a nice swimming hole. The kids just really enjoyed playing in that swimming hole . . . And they just got more fun out of making the girls scream! Boys always do that—you know that. And it was scary—but scary was fun. So we did hike over to the Emerald Pools, and we did hike up to the Weeping Rock—that was another favorite place.

One interviewee shared a magical family memory:

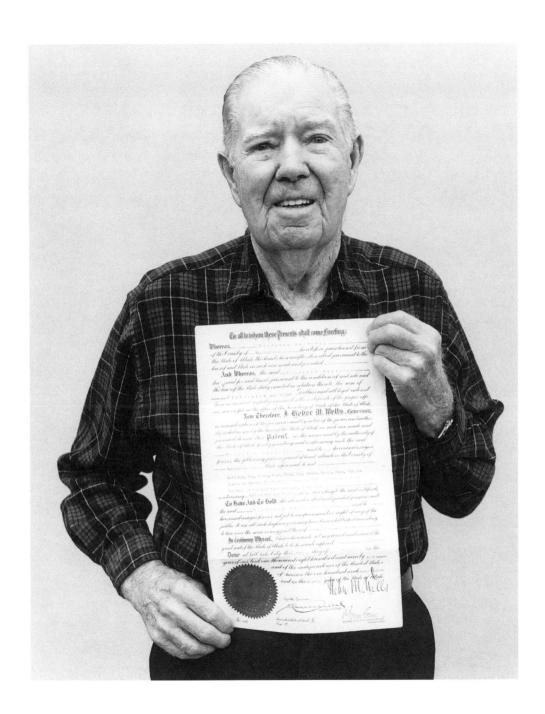

PHILIP HEPWORTH, BORN 1916, AND ORIGINAL 1899 LAND DEED

[Springdale] used to, as a town, go up to the upper campgrounds, the Grotto as it's called. It was open to the public then and we used to get together as a whole ward and just go up there on a wagon or in our pickups or whatever and have cookouts. I can remember one evening particularly, just being snuggled up against my father and he had his arm around me. I was just a little girl. And as that beautiful moon came up over those peaks in Zion, they began to sing *When the Moon Comes Over the Mountain* and I've never forgotten that. I felt so loved and so secure in that group that evening.

Another interviewee born two years before the establishment of the national park, discussed her feeling about Zion and the surrounding countryside:

We always, always enjoyed the park. . .I was always quite proud of . . . the fact [that I lived near Zion National Park]. It never occurred to me that someone wouldn't like the fact that there was a park there. I always thought [Zion] was always wonderful. I always liked the amenities that were there. I just thought that it was a great place to live. I felt we were pretty fortunate to have it. To be that close to a beautiful place like that. I felt that my brothers and sisters and parents felt the same way . . . I was always proud . . . "You know where Zion Park is . . ." It gave me some area reference to tell them where I came from.

Zion Pioneers and Spirituality in the Land of Zion

AS NOTED EARLIER, most of the residents of Zion Canyon during the Pioneer Voices era were members of the Church of Jesus Christ of Latter-day Saints. Much of their daily lives revolved around their spiritual beliefs, sense of family, and community connections. Philip Hepworth, born in 1916 in Zion Canyon, commented about how he felt they were perceived as Mormon settlers in relation to the land and the park:

About the religion connection . . . we went to church and practically everybody in Springdale belonged to the Mormon Church, they were LDS and it influenced their lives . . . We were like a big happy family . . . we were taught to work and be honest and thrifty and all of the virtuous things of life. We were taught that as we grew up . . . There was an erroneous rumor that went around for years. You used to hear that "the natives, they don't appreciate that park, we've got to get in there and preserve it so they don't destroy it. They want places to farm, they don't want a park to look at." But that was a mistaken idea. All the people I know . . . they loved that park. They loved those mountains . . . I've always, all my life I've continued to love nature and the outdoors because I grew up in it.

Hall (1999) affirms, "It is a generally accepted notion that the early Mormon settlers were blind to the beauties of Zion Canyon, their energies being directed to the task of extracting a livelihood from a hostile environment. Such was not the case" (p. 44).

A Pioneer Voices interviewee described the interaction between her ancestry and land ethic:

I'm proud of my pioneer heritage. These are the people who came and settled this part of the country. And they're strong people and I'm proud of that. I'm proud to be a part of that, those people. And they're what built this area up. And so I take pride in the fact that those were my ancestors, those were my people [who did] that. And when things don't look right or things get messed around I take it personally. You know . . . it means a lot to me, this area . . . I try to take care of my piece of the earth here. I try to remember my ancestors. I think that's one reason that I am so interested in genealogy and doing these histories . . . is because I admire those people so much.

Another pioneer interviewee noted the stereotype that he felt was incorrect of Mormon settlers as oblivious to the natural world around them:

The Mormons didn't attribute any spiritual . . . that is, "life" . . . to the mountains, like maybe the Native Americans do. You see they think everything has a spirit. I don't think we looked at the mountains [like that]. Though we admired them and were happy to live among . . . the mountains . . . A lot of people had the idea that the Mormons, the early settlers didn't appreciate the beauty of the area. And of course I think the reason is that they didn't have a lot to say about it and they didn't write about it very much. Because they were busy twenty-four hours a day making a living. And didn't have much time to lay around . . . however, I'm sure they did have an appreciation. A lot of people noticed well. Joseph Black who was one of the first settlers in there. He was a young man and he is evidently reputed to be the first one to hike on up the canyon beyond Springdale and come back raving about the beauty to the extent that people got to calling it "Joe's Glory." So somebody noticed the beauty.

Della Higley reaffirmed the pioneer link to the land. "I feel that the pioneers were in love with the canyon . . . I don't know—what you would call it. But they appreciated the land and they appreciated the beauty that was here."

Many of them did notice the beauty of the canyon in spite of their challenging lives in Zion. Alma Cox, born in 1919, commented:

I've always . . . thought about the beauties of nature and God's creations and . . . [it] always amazes me what the Lord has done when He's created this earth for us. And the park also. I remember when I was postmaster why, I was postmaster for a long, long time [in Rockville] and the tourists would come down . . . after they'd been up in the park and they'd have a bunch of cards that they had bought and they wanted 'em cancelled out so they could go to their homes and some of the people they come and [said], "Just a big pile of rocks," and others would [say], "Oh, it was magnificent! Magnificent, those

sheer ledges going up there." And you couldn't imagine . . . the difference in people! Ha, I guess it all depends on the eyes of the beholder I suppose . . . but most of 'em, most of 'em really enjoyed . . . one lady says, "This is just like being in the Celestial Kingdom." Well, she was talking about Rockville. She was talking about Rockville. "This is just like being in the Celestial Kingdom."

In addition, the lives of the Mormon settlers and the park intersected when it came to livelihood as well as philosophy. Betsy Alford, born in 1938 in Springdale, and her sister Janis Kali, born 1936, were interviewed for the Pioneer Voices Project and are both current Zion National Park employees. Descendants of a Mormon pioneer family, First Acting Zion Superintendent Walter Ruesch was their maternal grandfather, their paternal grandfather was District Supervisor of the Civilian Conservation Corps (CCC) and their father was Zion CCC foreman. They provided insight on how their heritage and spirituality were interconnected with a land ethic. Alford noted, "I think there's something spiritual myself that talks to you here [in Zion]. I've always felt it. I could be gone a day, I could be gone weeks, I could be gone years . . . but I keep coming back to the land, coming back to this area . . . it gathers you in and says 'okay, you're home and you're safe.' And I think part of that was because of grandpa [Walter Ruesch] . . . a very rough-spoken man and every other word was a swear word . . ."

Her sister Janis Kali continued, "I also remember [Grandpa's] great love for this park. He was a woodcarver and I remember he carved a sign . . . He nailed it up to one of the trees in the [Zion] campground and it said 'This is God's country. Don't make it look like Hell.' I think it was a mistake to take that down because it was a part of this history and it was a part of the way we felt about our connection to the land."

The daughter of chief ranger Donal Jolley, also of Mormon pioneer heritage, remembered how her father felt about protecting and preserving the park. When asked if they ever ate Sego lilies, as many settlers had, Lorna [Jolley] Kesterson replied:

No. My dad was pretty strict about what we were doing. I'll tell you this one story about my dad. They were making a movie up in Zion with Tom Mix and they had their cameras set up and there was one branch of a tree that was right in the way, so they kept after Dad to cut that down so they wouldn't have to move their camera. But he wouldn't do it. So Tom Mix offered him a cowboy hat if he'd cut that branch off but Dad wouldn't cut it and he didn't get the cowboy hat either. That's the way he was: very strict, strict with regulations.

An ethic of stewardship toward the natural world was a part of the Zion pioneer experience, even though this was often at odds with the fervent struggle to survive and persevere in what to the settlers surely seemed an unforgiving land. The pioneers derived lasting joy from the land and found an anchoring sense of place in its midst. If this historically-based sense of place and stewardship towards nature is acknowledged as integral to the Zion pioneer experience, it follows that responsibility to the natural world must also have an integral role in the heritage of Zion pioneers: for past, present and future. This acknowledgement can be beneficial both to the land of Zion and to its human inhabitants.

For the children who came of age in Zion from the 1910s–1930s, their own transition to adulthood was mirrored by the evolution of the cultural and natural world around them. A new national park signaled increasing federal control of land in Utah. This was accompanied by the onset of industrialization and urbanization, the shift from barter to a cash economy, and increased educational and job opportunities which led some canyon residents to move to other places. It also led to the decline of subsistence agriculture and the increasing presence of visitors and new residents in the canyon.

What stands out in the memories of Pioneer Voices Project interviewees about their childhood? Is it the advent of the new national park, the changing world outside, encroaching adulthood, or the exotic visitors to the canyon? Interestingly, many of the children who grew up in the early years of the park amidst the transition described one of the hallmarks of their youth as the *freedom* they felt in the Zion countryside:

The freedom to go up there in the hills. We climbed the rocks and searching for diamonds up there and all those beautiful rocks. You know when any of the grandchildren came to Rockville, they always went home with a bagful, a pocket-ful of rocks. And it was just a wonderful place to live. A wonderful place to live. I felt so fond [of it]. I always felt so fortunate to have been born there. As I've said many times, I must have been rewarded for having been born to goodly parents. It was a wonderful place to live . . . We slept outdoors in the summertime. That was a big thing, to have a bed outside. We all had beds outside . . . Oh, just out in the open air, you know, and the stars above and the good fresh smell of every-thing . . . I'm so used to color and living in southern Utah, you know, "color country" that I don't think anything's very pretty unless it's colorful. I remem-ber going through Wyoming and Montana, just these big plains and nothing but sagebrush and I thought, "Oh, there's just no color in this place . . ." I think it's so beautiful, looking out in Rockville, too, and seeing all of those beautiful mountains. Ah, the picture, it's just picturesque. Still, I'm so intrigued with it when I go back. I wish I could paint them. I think they're beautiful.

Sometimes, the stories about the freedom of their youth were humorous:

Oh, we run around like a bunch of wild people! Like I say, as kids usually do. We were out a lot. We'd be playing in the trees, playing in the rocks, climbing rocks, sometimes get up on one and couldn't get down! I had one cousin I played with a lot, she was older than I was, about two or three years older, but we played together a lot, and she was more of the tomboy. She'd climb a tree; if she could climb a tree, okay, then we'd climb it. If she could get up on a rock and thought it was okay for us smaller kids, we'd climb it. I remember once she couldn't get down! She'd slip and slide, she'd try to come down and, course, she took her shoes off, and then that rough sandrock hurt her feet so bad. We had to throw her shoes back up to her. And we threw and threw! It was all dark when she finally got off from that rock!

Other times, the tone of the stories reflected the idea that some of that freedom was ephemeral:

I wouldn't change my childhood with my grandchildren's childhood for anything in the world. It was a . . . gentler time, a slower time and we all knew each other. It was like a big family, our towns were in those days. And you watched out for each other. I just have nothing but wonderful memories of growing up in Springdale and being . . . close to the park where we could go in and out as we wanted to.

Another interviewee explained:

Well, the way I feel about [Zion Canyon] was that it was home, it was safe and . . . my family were here and we just felt at peace here. It was someplace that we thought we could worship God as we felt we should . . . we loved everyone that was here . . . I don't remember any real controversy that went on. If there was, it generally didn't affect me and my close family. And we felt at home here. We felt that this is where we're meant to be . . . I was raised in a spiritual family and . . . it made it easier for me to live my life as I feel like I should have lived it. It's a lot of examples to follow. My father was a quiet man, but he was a spiritual man also. I don't know what could have been better about my childhood.

Another pioneer mused on the transition from tradition to modernity in Zion Canyon:

They were very quiet years. But I know that, the people were very, very concerned with each other and for their animals. And we were very concerned about the wild animals because they would get the farm animals if they could. . . . And

. . . it was hard living here. . . . But the people loved the land and they loved the reason they were here. They took good care of everything that they had and not a thing was wasted. I think people lived closer to the land in those days . . . I won't say they worshipped the land—they respected the land. And they knew that it was the way they would make a living. And nowadays that isn't the way they make their living, and so they don't have the same relationship that they used to have.

That relationship was embodied for many of the pioneers by their sense of independence tempered with safety as children in Zion of yesterday:

We were so isolated, I guess, we didn't get out and learn the ways of the world. 'Cause we were very isolated here, maybe become too self-oriented. I don't know. But I think it did make a difference. 'Cause we were different from people who lived out in these bigger places. We just lived out in the sticks! We was hillbillies! [But] I'm glad I grew up here . . . I think it was good for us in a way. We had to make our own way. We learned to work hard and appreciate each other and we just learned to love this canyon. And so maybe that does have an effect on our whole lives, I don't know. I think it probably did. But we made our own entertainment, we made our own food, everything had to be pretty much what we could do our selves for a long, long time. . . .

All interviewees, like Barbara (Terry) Bell, born in Rockville in 1918, seemed to share in common a belief that their childhood in Zion was a cherished time:

Well, I'm sure that . . . having been raised in a small town, I think it's to my advantage as far as that goes. I can't see my dad doing anything else than what he did for a living [running the Rockville mercantile]. And while we weren't rich, we always had enough to eat and clothes to wear. So I don't ever regret not . . . having gone, you know, farther afield . . .

DAN CRAWFORD, BORN 1914

Another explained how the past tied into the present. "I've always felt that the people in this area have very strong spirits. Otherwise they wouldn't have been chosen to come down here in this desolate desert country. And they stuck it out here and raised their families and I've always been very, very proud of my pioneer heritage. When I think of what they went through so that I could have the life I've got now. "

The power of heritage and place continued to tug at many long after their childhood was over and the journey to adulthood was underway. One explained, "Well, it was great for me [living in Zion]. I always enjoyed it. When we left for employment purposes, like when I went to California, I was there a couple of years, I couldn't wait to get back to Zion. Same way when I was in the service for a year and eight months. Come back to Zion."

And "come back to Zion" many did. Sometimes, bringing their children and grand-children with them to share the joy.

One interviewee explained it thusly:

I've always enjoyed the out-of-doors. I've always enjoyed plants and flowers and . . . especially birds [and] animals. I don't do any hiking anymore; I don't have the ability to. But I think being acquainted with Zion and Cedar Mountain is what shaped me into what I am. And I have a granddaughter who I taught into the out-of-doors who wouldn't otherwise. You know, city girl, never get away from town . . . I used to take her with me up there [to Zion National Park]. That was many years later, of course. But it was because of how I had grown up. And the out-of-doors was always part of our life. And Zion was one of those important points in that.

Dan Crawford was born in 1914 in a cabin on Oak Creek. That cabin is gone and only traces remain of the irrigation ditches that once surrounded it. Children who once played there in the shadow of Steamboat Mountain are 90 years old now. Even the name of the mountain has changed. Today's visitors know it as the West Temple. Crawford summed up that moment in the history of Zion that was for him the world of childhood.

"I thought that every place in the world had mountains around, and I thought they all had a river running past. I grew up and enjoyed the land . . . Best place in the world, I guess . . . I assumed I'd always live there." Interviewee Philip Hepworth echoed this sentiment when he explained of his Zion Canyon childhood, "It was just a wonderful life . . . I'd kinda like to go back and live it over."

The name of the canyon, "Zion," means "sanctuary." It has served as such for animals, plants, and humans for centuries. The pioneers of Zion used natural resources to survive, and like all of us do every day, they left an imprint on the land. But the land left an imprint on them, as well. In a sense, we are all their descendants. We have inherited their history; their heritage is our lesson. Although families struggled with the land of Zion and its elements, they loved that land, and many of them never left it. Others who left it, have returned to it. All of them preserve it, at least in their memories. These Zion pioneers have more in common with those who came before and with we who came after, than they have differences. The land is a part of us and it always has been. And we still depend on it in many and complex ways, from its resources to its respite. Like the pioneers in their time of transition, those who care about Zion Canyon today strive to adjust to more visitors, more imprints on the land, and more challenges to natural resources from inside and outside the park boundaries than we have ever known before. The "pioneers" of today may be measured in how they respond to these challenges and the ensuing choices. Perhaps our best guide may be the voices of the pioneers that echo in Zion Canyon and remind us of what we have.

SOURCES CITED

Alder, D. D. and K. F. Brooks. 1996. *A History of Washington County: From Isolation to Destination.* Salt Lake City, Utah: Utah State Historical Society.

Brehm, J. M. and B. W. Eisenhauer. "Environmental Concern in the Mormon Culture Region." *Society and Natural Resources.* 19: 393–410.

Crawford, J. L. 1999. *Zion Album: A Nostalgic History of Zion Canyon.* Springdale, Utah: Zion Natural History Association.

Crawford, J. L. 2002. *Zion National Park: Towers of Stone.* Springdale, Utah: Zion Natural History Association.

Eves, R. L. 2005. *Water, Rock, and Time: The Geologic Story of Zion National Park.* Springdale, Utah: Zion Natural History Association.

Flores, D. 2001. *The Natural West: Environmental History in the Great Plains and Rocky Mountains.* Norman, Oklahoma: University of Oklahoma Press.

Garate, D. T. 2001. *The Zion Tunnel: From Slickrock to Switchback.* Springdale, Utah: Zion Natural History Association.

Larsen, W. 2004. *Indian and Pioneer Medicinal and Food Plants.* St. George, Utah: West Press.

Nelson, R. A. 1976. *Plants of Zion National Park: Wildflowers, Trees, Shrubs and Ferns*. Springdale, Utah: Zion Natural History Association.

St. George Chamber. 2006. Annual Growth Rate of Washington County. Retrieved May 12 from http://stgeorgechamber.com/demographicsprojections.htm

Toweill, D. E. 2003. *Desert Bighorn Sheep*. Palm Springs, California: Nature Trails Press.

Rhode, D. 2002. *Native Plants of Southern Nevada: An Ethnobotany*. Salt Lake City, Utah: The University of Utah Press.

Hall, V. *A History of Rockville*. 1999. Unpublished manuscript. Page citations correspond to computer manuscipt.

Warner, T. J., Editor. 1995. *The Dominguez-Escalante Journal*. Salt Lake City: University of Utah Press.

Winters, R. 2003. "Being Green in the Land of the Saints." *High Country News*. 35: 10–15. December 22, 2003.

Woodbury, A. M. 1997. *A History of Southern Utah and its National Parks*. Springdale, Utah: Zion Natural History Association.

Left to right: Michael Plyler, Eileen M. Smith-Cavros, and Lyman Hafen

EILEEN M. SMITH-CAVROS, Ph.D., was the founding director of the Zion Canyon Field Institute and is currently an environmental sociologist and assistant professor of sociology at Nova Southeastern University in Fort Lauderdale, Florida.

LYMAN HAFEN is executive director of Zion Natural History Association and the author of eight books on the history, landscape, people, and culture of southern Utah.

MICHAEL PLYLER is the current director of the Zion Canyon Field Institute and an award-winning photographer specializing in the dying art of black and white photography.

ABOUT ZION NATURAL HISTORY ASSOCIATION

This book is published by the Zion Natural History Association (ZNHA), a nonprofit corporation working in cooperation with Zion National Park. Publishing is just one of the functions we perform to enhance the quality of your visit to National Park Service areas. The association also funds interpretive projects and scientific research, produces free publications, aids in museum and library activities, awards scholarships, and helps with many other National Park Service programs. The Zion Canyon Field Institute has been created by ZNHA and Zion National Park, offering a variety of educational courses to children, students, adults and families.

ZNHA is directed by a voluntary board of directors and is supported by the sale of publications, maps, and other interpretive items that visitors can purchase at our visitor center sales areas and on our website. The association could not continue to assist the National Park Service without your support.

We invite you to consider becoming a member of Zion Natural History Association. For more information, you may access our website at www.zionpark.org, or call (800) 635-3959.